Keeping the Sabbath Today?

by Jay E. Adams

TIMELESS TEXTS
Stanley, North Carolina

Dedicated to
John Austin Younts
who read the manuscript and
offered numerous helpful suggestions.

Contents

Introduction

It is with some trepidation that I set out to write this book. A few of my friends will regret that I entered the lists. Others, some of whom have urged me to write, will rejoice. Because I surely will not please everyone, and because I know that I shall bring down the wrath of others upon my head, I want to make it clear from the outset that I understand something of what will come my way as the result of publishing this volume.[1] It is not that "Adams, in his dotage, has wandered afield in areas he should not have transgressed." No, it is only after full inner deliberation and knowledge of consequences that I write.

A Need To End Confusion

"But why do so if you know there will be negative consequences? Are you just being contrary?" No. I have waited long to write. This is not a recent decision. I have even refused to do so. But, as someone recently said, "You've got to write about this issue; there are so many persons who are confused. Please help them." A pastor loses a "Sabbath-keeping family" from his congregation because they heard a member of another family of the church say that he was going out to eat at a restaurant after a church service. A father agonizes over whether he ought to do anything other than attend church, play Bible games with the children, help the poor, sick, and needy, and read Christian literature on Sunday. May he turn on the television and listen to the news? May he watch any other sort of program? What may he do or not do?

---

1. Doubtless, F.W. Robertson was correct. He said, "It is very difficult to discuss this question of the sabbath. Heat, vehemence, acrimony are substituted for argument. When you calmly ask to investigate the subject, men apply epithets, and call them reasons; they stigmatize you as a breaker of the sabbath, pronounce you dangerous; with sundry warnings against you in private, and pregnant hints in public." In *Twenty Centuries of Great Preaching*, Vol. IV. Clyde Fant & William Pinson, eds. Word Books: Waco (1974), p. 387.

These are the sorts of questions that eat away at the hearts and minds of many sincere Christians. Where does a person draw the line? The fact that few Sabbath-keeping families have similar standards (unless they belong to a church where members march in lock step) also causes difficulty. Who's right? Who's wrong? Moreover, how does one apply Old Testament restrictions, rules and regulations today? Or, on the other hand, should he? In Palestine, one might easily get by without heat one day a week. But in a blustery northern area today, should one let his family freeze rather than throw wood on the fire or turn up the thermostat and thereby make others work? And what about attending church? Terry has no Bible-believing (let alone Reformed) congregation within walking distance. In order to attend one, should he take a bus, taxi or subway since he has no automobile? Why should others work to convenience him? How do the words of the Westminster Standards apply? How does one worship the whole time on Sunday differently from the way he does on other days? And is the first day of the week both the Lord's Day and the Sabbath as Question 117 of the Larger Catechism calls it? These, and a multitude of other questions arise as Christians seek to honor God in this matter.[1]

Recently, I was chagrined by attending a Sunday meal at the home of a Sabbath-keeper. The hostess had worked long and hard to prepare the meal. But she, and other Sabbath-keeping guests, seemed not to be bothered by that. Also, the conversation as we ate the delicious food that she provided roamed over a wide variety of topics – what people's backgrounds were, what they thought of different kinds of auto-

---

1. "Years ago…A. van Selms wrote that, on an average, ten thousand families in the Netherlands alone were affected by serious quarreling about what was, and what was not, permissible on Sunday." In J. Douma, *The Ten Commandments: Manual for the Christian Life.* P&R Publishing Company: Phillipsburg (1996), p. 146. That is how serious the question can become among those who care. In an uncaring society like ours today, proportionally the numbers may decrease, but the problem remains for those who truly want to serve God, but are perplexed.

mobiles – and it wasn't only the non-Sabbatarians who participated in the chit-chat. Most of us had driven three-quarters of an hour to attend this wonderful gathering, and would drive at least another three-quarters of an hour returning to our homes. The trips were tiresome rather than refreshing. I wondered about whether I should point out what seemed to me to be inconsistencies in such conversations and activities, but I remembered my wife's wise admonitions against doing such things and remained silent! Yet, all of the way home I mused about how anyone could keep the Old Testament Sabbath today.

It doesn't take long for an inquiring young believer to recognize that Christians are divided over what has come to be called "The Sabbath Question." Some think that the seventh day has been transmuted into the first day without appreciable differences between the two. In their view, all of the Old Testament regulations, with their accompanying encouragements, prohibitions and severe warnings pertain as fully to Christians as to Jews.[1] Some in this group make adjustments on the principle of general equity.[2] Still others, think the Sabbath day has been done away with along with the other Old Testament shadowy ceremonies and rituals. They see no biblical warrant for dividing civil and ceremonial law from moral law. Then, there is a great host of believers who simply don't know what to believe, who are totally perplexed about the question and who, as a consequence, agonize weekly about how to observe the first day of the week.

I have little hope of changing the minds of those in the first group. Besides, if they want to observe the day let them do so. Scripture certainly doesn't forbid it so long as they don't judge others who disagree (see Colossians 2:16). I may be able to reinforce the thinking of those in the second group and, perhaps, help them to better appreciate the views and practices of those in the first category. But it is for the third,

---

1. Perhaps with the exception of putting violators to death.
2. That is, adopting what they believe to be the functional equivalents.

especially, that I write. Having remained in limbo about this matter for so long myself, I can understand the confusion, uneasy feelings, and self-imposed guilt that they experience. Possibly this book will be used by God to free them from this weekly misery and help others from ever experiencing it.

Why Another Book?

When there are so many books written concerning the "Sabbath Question," why write another? That is a valid question. The simple answer is, frankly, for years people have asked me, "What book would it be helpful to read about the Sabbath?" I have been at a loss to answer. Throughout the years, I have voraciously devoured every book about the Sabbath that I could get my hands on; but again and again, coming to a new book with high hopes, I have had them dashed. In the worst way I wanted to find one with the answers for others and for myself. So – whether or not this book will serve that purpose – I send forth *Keeping the Sabbath Today?* with the prayer that God will use it as a blessing.

Some Freedom on the Question

Over the years, I have listened to Presbytery examinations in which men seeking ordination have expressed reservations about the Sabbatarian viewpoint set forth in the Standards of the Church. Regularly, they have been allowed to take an exception.[1] It seems that there would be many men refused admission if they didn't! I do not think that they have violated their ordination vows. Rather, I hope this book will help many men entering the ministry to vow with greater confidence.[2]

---

1. Upon uniting with my present Presbytery, I too was allowed to take an exception.
2. In sustaining the position of a Mr. Francis Breisch, the committee of the Presbytery of Wisconsin in the Orthodox Presbyterian Church that was elected to confer with him cited Charles Hodge's position that one who holds a view similar to Calvin's (which is essentially that which I espouse) "does not deny this system of doctrine [the Reformed Faith]...The doctrine

At any rate, admittedly this is a controversial volume. I write, however, not to stir up controversy, but to help those who wonder about the matter. I hope that it will not lead to serious friction over an issue that, until resolved, should be dealt with as a matter of indifference – the way the New Testament treats it:

> One person regards one day above another, day; another regards every day the same. Each person must become fully convinced in his own mind. The one who observes the day, observes it for the Lord, and the one who eats, eats for the Lord since he gives thanks to God...So then, each of us will give an account of himself to God. Therefore, we must stop judging one another. Rather, make this judgment – not to put a hindrance or a stumbling block in a brother's way.
>
> Romans 14:5, 6, 12, 13

We must all take Paul's word for it, since his word is Christ's Word!

---

concerning...the Sabbath...contains nothing peculiar to our system." *Church Polity*, p. 310. The committee adds, "Historically, all Presbyterian churches in this country have been willing to consider as applicants for the ministry men who differ at minor points with these standards, including differences regarding the Christian Sabbath" (mimeographed copy of the report to the Presbytery, n.d.).

CHAPTER ONE

Why Some Do Not Observe the Sabbath[1]

Let's begin right where we left off in the introduction. We were looking at Romans 14:5, 6, 12, 13. There Paul raised the issue. He expressed concern about how a Christian should properly relate to a weak brother with whom he disagrees (v. 1). One of the two matters that he used as an example was whether or not one might eat meat. He treated the question as a matter of indifference: a believer may or may not eat it according to his best understanding at the time. What counts, he says, is that whatever he does, he must do it "for the Lord" (v. 6). He is to do what he does for the honor of the Lord Jesus Christ. But Paul doesn't leave the matter there. He urges everyone to come to a proper understanding of the matter in such a way that he is fully persuaded that his practice is biblical (v. 5). Only then can he eat in faith what before he wondered about, and not sin (v. 23). And, in eating, he must do nothing that would lead another to violate his conscience (v. 13). He must put no stumbling blocks in his weak brother's way (v. 20). Moreover, he must not judge others when there is a difference of opinion about such issues. This matter of judging seems to be the overarching concern of the entire discussion.

In making the point that both those who eat and those who don't must do whatever they do for the Lord, he links the eating question with the keeping of days (vv. 5, 6). The two problems, he indicates, are similar. He puts them into the same category. Some Christians thought the keeping of days of the Jewish calendar was still necessary. (Surely Paul referred to Jewish "days." Pagan "days" could never be kept "for the Lord.") In the early days of the church there were many Jewish believers who had misgivings about leaving these "days" behind. So, during the time of transition before

---

1. The word "Sabbath" means a period of "cessation and rest."

70 AD Paul says that whether you keep the day or not is, in itself, not all that important so long as you do so to the Lord and don't judge brothers who do otherwise. It seems that there was no need to further explicate the matter for the Romans, but only to refer to the problem, since the Christians there were familiar with it and, presumably, some were struggling with it. Doubtless, there was difficulty (just as there is today) concerning Sabbath-keeping – one of those "customs" mentioned by James and the brothers who gathered at Jerusalem to confer about such issues (Acts 15).

"Days" and the Sabbath Issue

"Yes," you say, "but what do those verses have to do with the Sabbath Question?" They have everything to do with it. There are those in the church today who want to keep the weekly Sabbath because they think that Scripture *requires* them to do so. They want to be true to their Lord. Fine, so long as they don't judge others who disagree with their view and don't place a stumbling block before anyone. Let them keep the Sabbath until they become otherwise persuaded in their own minds. "Well, the passage doesn't specifically mention the Sabbath," you may observe. Yes, that's correct; but when referring to keeping a Jewish "day" it doesn't exclude it either! And *that* is significant.

"How so?" No exceptions are made to the "days" that one may or may not keep. If it were of great importance for Christians to continue to observe the weekly Sabbath, Paul should have distinguished between it and some other days (if, indeed, he had other days in mind, as some think). But he didn't. You don't clarify a doubtful situation with vague, non-specific references. Since the word "days" is general enough to include the most common day (the weekly Sabbath), it was incumbent upon Paul to exclude it in some way or another if he meant to. But he made no distinction. And, once again, in Colossians 2:16, 17 (after telling his readers that the "requirements" of the Old Testament law had been "taken away," v. 14), he writes in summary of his previous discussion:

> So then, you must allow nobody to judge you
> about eating and drinking or about feasts or new
> moons or sabbaths, which are shadows of what
> was coming (the body belongs to Christ).

Again, Paul links eating and the observance of days. But here, in contrast to that in Romans, significantly, his reference is more specific. Here, he lists the days that he has in mind: feasts, new moons and sabbaths. What does he mean by this list?

Again, No Distinction

Well, it's plain that once more Paul failed to distinguish the shadowy sabbaths he had in mind from any others. There are those who think he was referring to one of the special sabbaths mentioned in the Old Testament that were distinct from the weekly sabbaths.[1] But, no, that isn't what he said. He simply said "sabbaths."

If Paul wanted Christians to keep the weekly Sabbath, he surely missed a golden opportunity to stress the fact. He could have said, "Now you understand, of course, I'm not referring to the Sabbath that we all keep every week." But the fact is, he said no such thing. He said "sabbaths." Since he made no such distinction, the weekly Sabbath, therefore, is the day that would most naturally come to mind. If Paul didn't mean the weekly Sabbath, once again we must conclude that he muddied waters that were already murky enough. But Paul wasn't one to muddy anything! His meaning is perfectly clear. If there is uncertainty about his words it is we, not Paul, who have mucked things up.

To what does verse 16 refer? And how can we be sure that Paul was calling the *weekly* Sabbath a shadow that has passed at the appearance of the body that cast it? The verse itself pro-

---

1. Sabbatarians think the word "sabbaths" in verse 16 may refer to the yearly feasts mentioned in Leviticus 23. But this could not be, since the word "feast" in the Colossians passage distinguishes these annual feasts from the weekly Sabbath. The two are clearly distinguished, and both are included in this verse by the apostle.

vides the answer. Notice, carefully, Paul lists three categories of days:

1. First, the *annual* feasts, like the Feast of Tabernacles;
2. Second, the *monthly* feasts of the New Moon;[1]
3. Third, as you would expect in the sequence, the *weekly* Sabbath.

This comprehensive succession includes *all of the days* of the Jewish calendar. To think otherwise would require what we don't have: a distinction of some sort or another indicating that the weekly Sabbath is not included in the list. Those who seek to make a distinction that just isn't there simply assume too much. Their view goes against a normal reading of the passage. Now, if this explanation (which should be sufficient in itself) helps to introduce Sabbatarians to the reason why non-Sabbatarians understand the Sabbath question as they do, there is more. Read on. We have but scratched the surface. Here, Paul says that the days were but a shadow that passed away when the body that cast it (Christ) appeared. Is He not our rest? How could non-Sabbatarians be satisfied with the shadow when they have the Substance? So, their reason for non-observance is that the Bible doesn't require them to. Why doesn't it? Because the Bible teaches that the Sabbath has been abolished.[2]

---

1. The Christian is no more obligated to keep the Sabbath than to observe the Feast of the New Moon. Indeed, if Isaiah 66:23 refers to New Testament times (as many think), then Henry Cowles was correct when he wrote, "It would seem that he himself [Isaiah] could not have thought of their coming up literally to worship God in *Jerusalem*; all flesh; every sabbath day." If the Sabbath and the Feast of the New Moon are not figurative, then the church would be expected to observe not only the weekly Sabbath, but the Feast of the New Moon as well. The two stand or fall together. It should be clear that it would be impossible for "all flesh" to come up to Jerusalem each week to observe the Sabbath! So, the passage plainly presents a picture of Gentiles keeping Sabbath *figuratively*.

2. Commenting on John 5:17, Calvin wrote, "It is true that the ceremony of the Sabbath was a part of the shadow of the law, and Christ put an end to it by His coming, as Paul shows (Colossians 2:17)."

CHAPTER TWO

Wasn't the Day Changed?

"Now wait a minute! Let's not move so quickly. I have been led to believe that the Sabbath was *not* abolished as you said at the conclusion of Chapter One. Instead, I was taught that there was simply a change of the day from Saturday to Sunday and that, in most other respects, it is the same. The change in days had to do with the fact that we now commemorate the Lord's resurrection on the first day of the week. My understanding is that we are to keep a *Christian* Sabbath."

You have been taught what many others also have been taught. But let me say it up front: there isn't the slightest indication that the Sabbath was ever changed from one day to another. That notion, which lies at the base of much wrong thinking, cannot be found in the Bible. One may search the Scriptures all the way through to the maps, but he will find nothing of the sort. The bold assertion of a change of day that entails a continuation of sabbatical requirements is made over and over again – but always apart from solid biblical argumentation. It is largely assertion, as I said, nothing more. But whoever asserts something is obligated to produce evidence for it. Where is it?

There is No Evidence

The reason I have so strongly emphasized the fact that it is unbiblical to teach that the day for observing the Sabbath was changed from Saturday to Sunday is because of its utter importance. Those who hold to the day-change view surely must offer evidence for this crucial assertion. Apart from it, all they claim is lost. Yet, in spite of this glaring omission – apart from any evidence whatever – the view is widely taught and accepted. Indeed, it is so commonly held in the English speaking Christian world that to even question it perplexes many who, in sheer disbelief, ask, "How could you think otherwise?"[1] But let me challenge you. Why don't you stop reading right now and search the Scriptures for the evidence behind the day-change view?

OK. Now that you have returned from your vain search for biblical proof, having found nothing of the supposed change in the Scriptures, perhaps you are better prepared to think seriously about the matter with an open mind. I hope so. Simply because something has been said over and over again does not make it so. Assertion, as you know, is not proof. There was a time when most people believed the earth is flat. But when the data came in, they had to change their minds (although I have heard of a small group called the Flat Earth Society who stick to the belief against all of the evidence).[2] It was this utter lack of evidence for the supposed change that weighed heavily upon my mind and, among other facts, led me to rethink my earlier position. Along with the crowd, I too had accepted the unfounded assertion.

Omissions are a Problem

I want *you* to think about this question for a moment. You are asked to believe, merely on the basis of assertion, that a momentous event occurred. But such an assertion is based merely upon the tradition of one group of Christians who, unlike those of other strains of believers, came to believe it. Their assertion, at best, is based upon inferential reasoning from data three or four steps removed from the conclusion. Their inferences are far too weak to accept. The fact of the matter is that not only is there no biblical evidence for such a change, there is a complete absence of any New Testament

---

1.   According to the Augsburg Confession, "The Scripture, which teacheth that all Mosaical ceremonies can be omitted after the Gospel is revealed, has abrogated the Sabbath." Philip Schaff, who held the opposite opinion, in a footnote admitted, "This view of the Christian Sabbath…was held by all of the Reformers." Philip Schaff, *The Creeds of Christendom*, Vol. III. Grand Rapids: Baker Book House (1990), p. 69.

2.   There will be those who maintain almost any belief that they find comfortable. They fear change.

command for the church to keep the Sabbath. Don't forget these two important omissions.

Why Only Nine?

Think of the facts. The other nine commandments are clearly reiterated in one form or another in the New Testament books. The sabbath commandment is not. Its absence is conspicuous. Strangely, there are those who argue that because nine out of the Ten Commandments may be found we must presume that the tenth is commanded as well. The strange thing is that they fail to focus on the significance of the *omission*! Because of the omission, one should ask, wouldn't you suppose, "Is there, perhaps, something different about the fourth commandment?" Indeed, we shall see later that there is such a difference.

No Additional Burden

Moreover, as we search the New Testament, we encounter other facts that tend to strengthen the idea that there is great significance in the lack of data about the supposed Sabbath change. Take, for instance, the Jerusalem decree of Acts 15:28:

> It seemed good to the Holy Spirit and to us not to lay any additional burden on you than these essentials: abstain from idol sacrifices, from blood, from strangled animals and from sexual sin. If you keep yourselves from these things, you will do well. Farewell.

Here, again, in this decree for the Gentile churches, the glaring absence of any mention of the Sabbath is apparent. The discussion from which this statement arose had to do with Jewish practices that must be required of Gentile converts. Since this was a declaration about the holdover of Jewish practices, you would expect the list to include Sabbath-keeping if it were required. Again, it is *conspicuously* absent. In the Old Testament, the Sabbath seems to have been accorded at least as high a place as the other items listed in verse 28. Yet, to those who hold the day-change view, it should come as

7

a surprise that it is not included among the other items. After all, the controversy over circumcision, having been successfully resolved, is then extended to other matters having to do with the keeping of "Moses' law" (v. 5). The conclusion that the Sabbath was not enjoined upon Gentile believers seems inevitable since the council declared that the list of items was complete: "It seemed good to the Holy Spirit and to us not to lay any additional burden on you" (v. 28). *No other burden.* No Sabbath. Another omission!

Before Sinai

Other ordinances that were included in the Mosaic Law, but were not observed *prior* to the formation of a theocratic kingdom at Sinai, did not have to be followed *after* the Mosaic period had run its course. It seems apparent that this was true of the Sabbath. The Mosaic Covenant was "added" to the Abrahamic Covenant – for a time. Its observance was never intended to be of perpetual duration and force (Galatians 3:19). Some Sabbatarians maintain that the Sabbath commandment is binding today because it was to be observed "throughout" Israel's generations and it was "perpetual" and "forever" (Exodus 31:16, 17). However, the same is said of other things, such as the Passover (Exodus 12:14). This is true only in that Christ is our Passover (I Corinthians 5:7; see also Genesis 17:7; Exodus 29:42; Leviticus 23:21). Today, Christ is our spiritual rest. Calvin wrote,

> Whatever was spoken of under the law as eternal, I maintain to have had reference to the new state of things which came to pass at the coming of Christ, and thus the eternity of the Law must not be extended beyond the fullness of time, when the truth of the shadows was manifested, and God's covenant assumed a different form…Besides, the Sabbath, although its external observation is not now in use, still remains eternal in its reality, like circumcision. Thus the stability of both was best continued by their

abrogation; since if God now required the same of Christians, it would be putting a veil over the death and resurrection of His Son...There is nothing which more completely confirms its reality and substance than the abolition of its external use.[1]

In his insightful commentary on Hebrews, Frederic Rendall of Cambridge wrote,

> By connecting God's new covenant in Christ directly with the original covenant made with Abraham, and declaring the Gentile believers to be children of Abraham and heirs of the promises made to the fathers, he [Paul] ignored the authority of the law of Moses. He treated the law as an incidental and temporary addition, almost of the nature of an interruption of God's original covenant (Galatians 3:19) – necessitated by man's transgressions, and therefore just and necessary, but still an interruption.[2]

During the entire patriarchal period, there is no record of Sabbath-keeping.[3] That was not because of laxity on the part of pre-Mosaic saints, but because they had no command to observe the day. When the Mosaic law was abolished, on this respect, all reverted to the time prior to its inception: God no more requires us to keep the Sabbath than He required the Patriarchs to do so.

---

1. *The Four Books of Moses, Vol. 1.* Baker Book House: Grand Rapids (1979), pp. 443, 444.
2. Rendall, Frederic. *The Epistle to the Hebrews.* London: Macmillan & Co. (1888), pp. 28, 29.
3. If the Sabbath were a "creation ordinance," as has been asserted, it should have been enjoined and observed throughout the period from Adam to Moses. But there is no evidence of any such observance. It was the founding of the Mosaic theocracy that gave occasion to such laws as the Sabbath (cf. Deuteronomy 12:8–10). It is not found in Genesis 2, though some Sabbatarians erroneously assert that it is implied.

Even on the occasion of the giving of manna, where a Sabbath of sorts was kept, nothing was said of keeping a full-fledged Sabbath (with restrictions on all labor). The Israelites were merely told to gather twice as much manna on the day before Saturday in order to observe what may have been a sort of preview of the Sabbath to be introduced at Sinai.[1] Again, if the day-change view were true, and the Sabbath were an enactment in force, we would expect the reason why manna would fall only six days a week would be clearly related to the Sabbath. And, it would pertain not only to manna-gathering, but also to all their activities. Yet, once more, just at the crucial point where it would have been entirely appropriate, no such explanation or command was forthcoming. The Sabbath (rest period) they were to observe had only to do with the gathering of manna. The people were not commanded to rest from any other activity. And Moses, who of all people ought to know, said, "The Lord did not make this covenant with our fathers, but with us, *at Horeb*" (Deuteronomy 5:3, emphasis mine). We are also expressly informed that the laws of the Mosaic Covenant were given to be kept "in the land" (Deuteronomy 4:14).

A Failure to Reprimand?

Never, it seems, did the Sabbath have application to pre-Sinai Israel, to the "fathers," or to any other people than those who came under the regulations of the Mosaic Covenant. Indeed, the Gentile nations were condemned for many sins, but we do not find them condemned for failing to keep the Sabbath as a creation ordinance. And, significantly, in the

---

1. Nehemiah's words are instructive: He says that God gave "impartial ordinances, reliable instructions and good decrees and commandments" (Nehemiah 9:13, HCSB). Continuing to speak of the giving of the law at Sinai, he says, "You [God] revealed Your holy Sabbath to them" (v. 14, HCSB)). Clearly in this verse we see that God's people learned about the Sabbath at the time of the giving of the law – not before. It is curious that, in his prayer, Nehemiah separated the Sabbath from the "commandments" given at Sinai as a ceremony that in some respect stands alone. Could he have considered it as distinct from the other nine in some respects?

New Testament lists of sins, which are quite complete (e.g., II Timothy 3:1ff.), again we find no trace of the sin of Sabbath-breaking. Most of the New Testament churches to which Paul wrote, and to which Jesus dictated His letters (Revelation 2, 3), were riddled with problems. But not once did either writer (or any other) mention failure to keep the Sabbath as one of them.[1] Nor were these congregations ever – not even once – exhorted to keep the Sabbath. Is it possible that none of these otherwise frequently disobedient Christians had no need of such exhortation? Once more, absence speaks more loudly than words!

When the Israelites came to Sinai, we read, "At that time "His voice shook the earth." Now, in the forthcoming destruction of Jerusalem that would finally bring an end to the old order, He promised that He would shake things up once more (Hebrews 12:26). The writer of Hebrews comments, "Now, 'once more' indicates the removal of what is shaken (created things, that is), so that what can't be shaken may remain" (v. 27). Only that which could not be shaken would remain. A shaking came at the inception of both the old and the new orders of things. We now have received "an unshakable kingdom." The question is what was shaken and what remains? It seems clear that the old, temporal and material things would pass away so that only those spiritual things which constitute the kingdom of Christ that it signified remain (see John 18:36). Types, ceremonies, days, and the like were not part of the new order. What passed away was removed by the upheaval also pictured in Acts 2:17–21.

---

1. J. Kenton Parker echoes the sentiments of many Sabbatarians: "Perhaps no command in the Decalog is more openly and frequently violated." *The Southern Presbyterian Journal*, Weaverville: April 30, 1952, pp. 7, 8. Strange indeed, if this is true, that we read nothing – nothing mind you – in the New Testament epistles of such violations in that day! Those churches, with all their many other flaws, must have had an extraordinarily successful record in this regard! Were they more righteous than we today? To ask is to answer the question!

CHAPTER THREE

A Code Disassembled?

It is striking that the command to keep the Sabbath does not occur in the New Testament, even though, in one form or another, the other nine do. Just as it is the only commandment of the ten that is said to be a "sign," (as we shall see later) so too in this way it appears unique. There is little question that, as the words of Nehemiah indicate, it stands apart from the rest.

Indeed, when you look at commandments in the New Testament, they no longer appear as a code of laws. There is no longer a unified *body of laws* like the "Ten Commandments." The code, as such, is gone.[1] There are but nine commandments (to which we can refer only with a small "c") mixed freely here and there with other commandments. They no longer stand out from among other rules and regulations as part of a code; their form as a unified code has disappeared. The removal of the fourth commandment, it seems, has played a part in destroying their arrangement as a codified group of laws.

A New Designation Found

Instead, beginning with Matthew 28:20, you read throughout the New Testament of *Christ's* commandments, rather than the Ten Commandments. And these are not codified, as were the Ten. Such a codification of laws was necessary for a temporal theocracy to serve as its constitution,[2] but now that there is no such theocracy, the need for such a constitution has passed. At any rate, there is no unified body of New Testament laws as there was in the Old Testament.

---

1. This fact accords with Galatians 4:24, 25. Viewed *as a whole*, the law was a guardian to lead God's people to Christ. But now that He has come, the need for the guardian has ceased.
2. The tables of the law, as the central element comprising the Mosaic Covenant, were placed in the Ark, which thereafter was appropriately

The New Testament speaks differently about God's commandments. It is significant that throughout it refers to *Christ's* commandments. The commandments of Christ, which are never codified, are summed up in one grand commandment, to "love." James calls this the royal law" (James 2:8). Jesus said, "If you love Me, keep My commandments" (John 14:15). When identifying the "greatest" commandment (and the one that ranks only second to it) Jesus didn't suggest that it was to keep the Sabbath, or – for that matter – any one of the Ten Commandments. Rather He focused on the second of the two summary commandments that, He said, encompass all of the Law and the Prophets (see also Galatians 5:6, 14). These, of course, were commands to love. And, we must not forget that John wrote,

> …we know that we love God's children: when we love God and keep His commandments. This is the love of God: that we keep His commandments, and His commandments aren't annoying.
>
> I John 5:2, 3

In this context, though at first it might seem that John refers to the Father's commandments, the words "His commandments" actually mean Jesus' commandments. We know this because John's words echo Matthew 11:30: "My yoke is easy to wear and My burden is light."[1] Moreover, in I John 2:3, we read, "By this we know that we have come to know Him – if we keep His commandments." Whose commandments? Verses 1 and 2 show contextually that it is Jesus' commandments that are in view. John also said, "This is love – that we walk according to His commandments," and then went on

---

referred to as "The Ark of the Covenant." That is, the Ark that contains the Covenant. That it is also called the "Ark of the Testimony" has to do with the fact that the people ratified the covenant (summarized in the Ten Commandments). The enclosure of these tablets bore witness (testimony) to this ratification. See Deuteronomy 31:26.

1. Note also Romans 7:6,"But now we are released from the law, dead to what firmly held us in its grip, so that we might serve in the newness of the Spirit and not in the oldness of the letter."

referring to Jesus' commandment: "This is the command-ment, even as you heard from the beginning – that you must walk in love" (II John 6). He also wrote,

> Dear friends, it isn't a new commandment that I am writing to you, but an old commandment that you had from the beginning; the old com-mandment is the Word that you heard. From another point of view, however, I am writing to you a new commandment that is true in Him and in you..." I John 2:7, 8

What John had in mind was the original preaching of the Word that his hearers "heard" and believed at the beginning of their Christian experience. This apostolic message, then, corresponds to Jesus' commission to the apostles to win con-verts and to teach them to "observe" (keep) *His* command-ments (Matthew 28:20). He does not say, "Keep the Ten Commandments."[1] Keeping Jesus' commandments was a part of the apostolic teaching that new converts received. The "aim" of this instruction was love (I Timothy 1:5). But it is certain that Jesus never commanded that the Ten Command-ments (or Ten Words) be observed as a codified law of His kingdom. Paul's concept of his ministry, found in II Corin-thians 3, confirms what he says in I Timothy. (See II Corin-thians 3:6–15, especially v. 9 where he contrasts the ministries of the Old and New Covenants.)

The "new commandment" that was "old"[2] was new in that for the first time someone kept it perfectly (John 13:34, 35;

---

1. Of course, since nine were repeated in the New Testament in various forms, they were to be observed as a part of Jesus' requirements. But they were not to be kept as a codification, or constitution, as the Mosaic theo-cratic law was. Moreover, the Bible knows nothing of the modern three-fold division of law as moral, judicial and civil. All of God's commandments are moral; to disobey any of them is sin.
2. It was found in Leviticus 19:18 (see also Romans 13:9). There is no three-fold division of the Law into judicial, civil and moral. They are all moral in that to disobey any is sin.

15:14). By doing so, Jesus provided a plain example of what love means.

Moreover, John says that *God's* "commandment" is that we should "believe in the Name of His Son Jesus Christ and love one another as He [Jesus] commanded us" (I John 3:23). And Paul speaks of "faith working through love" (Galatians 5:6). From these passages, there seems to be but one conclusion that one could reach: Jesus' "code," if you could call it such, is "Love" (see Galatians 5:6, 14). Indeed, Paul wrote, "Whoever loves the other person has fulfilled the law" (Romans 13:8).

Now, this "love code" is not amorphous, as some suppose. It is fulfilled as one "observes" Jesus' commandments (Matthew 28:20). There is, however, nothing to even intimate a one-to-one identity between the Ten Commandments as code and Jesus' commandments. It is clear, however, that – often in different form – nine of these commandments are found scattered *among* Jesus' commandments. All too obviously, for those who want to continue to observe the Mosaic code, the fourth commandment is plainly missing from them.

There seems to be little doubt, then, that beyond the references to the Sabbath in the Gospels (at the time when Jesus and those He addressed were still under obligation to keep the Old Testament law) post-Pentecostal preaching and teaching directs us to Jesus' commandments, not to the old code.

CHAPTER FOUR

But a Sabbath Remains
Christians Must Keep the Sabbath

Yes, even though the Sinaitic order of things has been shaken so as to remove what can be shaken (Hebrews 12:27), there is a Sabbath that remains – one that can *not* be shaken. Indeed, it is a Sabbath that is essential to salvation. I am not referring to observing Saturday, or even a once-in-every-seven-days rest. This enduring Sabbath is in heaven! In chapters three and four of his book, the author of Hebrews discussed the matter.

The main purpose of the Letter to the Hebrews was to convince Jewish converts that they did not make the wrong decision when they became Christians. Because they had come to experience some minimal persecution for their faith (12:4), some were wondering whether they ought to have left Judaism. Hebrews is a strong case for the correctness of their decision. In it the writer shows that what they have in Christ is far better than what they left behind. He wanted them also, like the fathers of old mentioned in chapter 11, to see that God's way is far better even if it does involve suffering. That is because God's way leads to heaven.

In making the argument that Christianity offers something better, the author of Hebrews sharply contrasts the old era with the new. The old is so inferior to the new that there is peril in abandoning the newfound faith that they had professed (see especially chapters 3, 4, 6, 10). To drift back into Judaism was to demonstrate that they did not possess the attributes that accompany salvation (6:9). Not only would their faith be proven false, but they would discover how "fearful" it is "to fall into the hands of the living God" (10:31). So, as a consequence, the entire book is peppered with strong warnings and earnest exhortations.

In chapter three, the writer shows how Jesus is greater than Moses since He is a Son over the house in which Moses only served. Today, Christians are that house (3:6). That is to say, we are such "if we hold firmly to the confidence and pride that we have in our hope" (3:6). Upon striking the note of warning found in the last verse, the writer makes an impassioned plea for his readers to be certain of their faith. The plea takes up all of chapter three and much of chapter four. What follows explains what he said and how it pertains to the Sabbath.

Perseverance Needed

The teaching "once saved, always saved" is correct, but incomplete. The phrase, "the perseverance of the saints" better states the truth because it includes human responsibility. Genuine, graciously given faith will always enable one to persevere to the end, but *he* must do it. To stress the point, the writer refers to Psalm 95:7–11, where David urges the reader not to "harden his heart" as the Israelites did in the desert. The quotation ends, "So I swore in My anger, 'they will not enter My rest'" (HCSB). It is that sentence that the writer goes on to expound and apply to the reader, ringing the changes on it over and over again.

He warns about hardening their hearts to the truth. Hardened hearts will turn them "away from the living God" (3:12). But, typically, he follows such warnings with an exhortation like this: "encourage one another every day, as long as we can still call it 'today' so that none of you will become hardened by sin's deceiving ways" (v. 13). For some, there would be no tomorrow; they would die before the sun dawned again. For others, the word "today" meant the time before going to meet their Lord. They must believe before it is too late.

There was no excuse for hesitating. The invitation was to believe – now. If they held to their original profession of faith in Christ, their assurance would be bright and clear. But, for some, doubts were creeping in. They were finding it difficult to square persecution with their new beliefs. Sin's deceitful ways had surfaced, and it was all too tempting to return to the more peaceful life of Judaism. They must abandon all doubt while it was still "today."

Just in Case

Just in case there were some with "unbelieving hearts," the writer worked out the fearful implications of the warning in Psalm 95. Those who "revolted" against Moses had been redeemed from Egypt, but never reached the promised land where they would find the greater "rest" from slavery. Sadly, their corpses were scattered over the desert because of unbelief (see also I Corinthians 10:6–10; II Peter 2:1; Jude 5).

Continuing his plea in chapter four (there were no chapter headings in the original), the writer again expresses his concern about the matter. His argument could be summed up this way:

> Be certain that all of you have believed and that none of you rebel as the Israelites did. If you do, you will fail to reach God's greatest rest. So, bring yourselves up short; make it your prime concern to enter into that rest.

The Fathers heard the message of eternal life through faith in the coming Messiah (Hebrews 11:13–16, 24–26, 38–40) and some believed. But for many the message was of no benefit because of lack of faith. The author of Hebrews sets forth their failure in terms that sound much like a chemical reaction in which an essential element is missing: they failed to "mix" faith with the Word (4:2).

Unlike them, readers who believe enter that rest. What God calls "My rest" is the rest that God Himself enjoys! God's faithful people will enter into it in the greater promised land (4:3). But unbelievers will never enter. Then comes a seemingly strange tag, hooked on to verse 3: "even though His works had been completed from the foundation of the world." This speaks of God finishing His work of creation, when on the seventh day He rested. What is its intent?

God rested from His works as Moses told us in his account of creation. Knowledge of the fact, then, isn't recent. Entering

19

into the heavenly rest has been a known reality for those with faith since the beginning of the human race. God's rest – which He enjoys – is perfect and complete. So, entering into His glorious rest (a message known all along) is a possibility that is still open to man (v. 6). In verse 7 the author quotes David's words urging them to take advantage of that window of opportunity while it is still "today."

The Rest That Remains

In case there could be any confusion, the writer makes it clear that the rest which David spoke of was not the rest that Joshua led his people into in the promised land of Canaan. This is clear, he says, because David, writing long afterward, still urged people to enter into God's rest. This fact plainly indicates that there is another Sabbath-rest (vv. 8, 9). It is the only Sabbath-rest that remains – the heavenly rest. When a believer enters that rest, like God, he too will rest from his labors. Obviously, a one-day-in-seven-rest can never be the true rest that is like God's rest. It brings no final rest to weary, sin-burdened Christians. In the heavenly Sabbath they shall find eternal *shalom* [peaceful rest].[1] In II Thessalonians 1:7, Paul refers to this heavenly rest in just that way. He says God will "give you rest...at the revelation of the Lord Jesus from the sky with His mighty angels." Hebrews 4, then, is a final exhortation for all to be sure of their salvation while it is still "today."

So, in these chapters there is no command to observe an earthly, weekly Sabbath. Something far greater is in view. This rest is the "homeland" – the "heavenly one"– that is better than the land of Canaan (Hebrews 11:14–16). In Revelation 14:13, the lot of the martyrs, "who die in the Lord," is said to be "rest from their labors." That heavenly country in which we shall find perfect rest is pictured in symbolic detail

---

1. Herman Hoeksema writes, "This entering into God's perfected work, into his rest, his Sabbath, is the idea of the Sabbath according to Scripture." *New Horizons,* Vol. 24, No. 3, OPC: Willow Grove, March (2003), p. 9.

in Revelation 21 and 22. It is to enter into blessed fellowship with the Lamb. Now *that* is rest.

The essence of the coined term used in Hebrews 4:9 is caught by Frederic Rendall who wrote:

> The employment of the term *sabbath rest* in a purely spiritual sense without comment or explanation, marks considerable progress in the spiritual interpretation of sabbatical language since the teaching of Christ, and indicates apparently a decay of the literal observance among Hebrew Christians.[1]

By failing to recognize this fact, one is in danger of missing the true intent of the author. It would be well, rather, to take to heart the words of the Heidelberg Catechism which beautifully catch the intent of the writer of Hebrews: "...all the days of my life I rest from evil works, allow the Lord to work in me by His Spirit, and thus begin in this life the everlasting Sabbath."[2] The summary of the passage by John Calvin, perhaps says it all: "To be short, the rest that God commands us is everlasting."[3]

1. *The Epistle to the Hebrews*. Macmillan & Co.: London (1888), p. 39.
2. In Philip Schaff, *The Creeds of Christendom*, Vol. III. Baker Book House: Grand Rapids (1990), p. 345.
3. *Sermons on Deuteronomy*. Banner of Truth: Edinburgh (1987), p. 203.

CHAPTER FIVE

The Sabbath and the Ten Commandments

An Important Change

Having examined the only New Testament passage in which we are urged to enter into a Sabbath rest, and having found it does not refer to an earthly Sabbath, what must we consider next? Doubtless, the matter that is yet a question in many minds has to do with the Ten Commandments. We have already explored some facts about them; here we intend to look at more.

People frequently ask, "If the other nine commandments are for us today, how is it that the fourth is not? Why is it an exception?" For many years that was *the* question that kept me from viewing the Sabbath commandment as fulfilled in Christ. Perhaps, too, this is the one obstacle you must hurdle to reach that conclusion. I shall now attempt to set your mind at ease about this seemingly insuperable problem.

For the Church Today?

The solution to the apparent problem may be found by recognizing that the Bible does not teach that the Ten Commandments – as given at Sinai – are for the church to observe. Nowhere is there any such command. Quite to the contrary; we saw that Scripture plainly affirms that they were given exclusively to Israel to keep. We know this because they are said to have been given to Israel at Sinai at the establishment of a covenant that, for a limited time, was grafted onto the Abrahamic Covenant. We know also that this added covenant was eventually abolished (Jeremiah 31:31) and that Christians are not a part of it. But they are still under the Abrahamic Covenant in its New Testament expression. The terms of that covenant promised that in Abraham's Seed, Jesus Christ, *all* nations of the earth would be blessed. Here are several references to this fact:

> I will bless those who bless you...and all the peo-
> ples on earth will be blessed through you.
>
> Genesis 12:3, HCSB

> ...in Him all the nations of the earth will be
> blessed.   Genesis 18:18

> And in your seed all the nations of the earth will
> be blessed.   Genesis 22:18

(See also Galatians 3:8, 9, 16; Acts 3:25.)

There is, then, nothing exclusive or temporary about the Abrahamic Covenant as there was about the Mosaic. From the outset we are told of its far-reaching application. It was adapted to every culture and clime. It was intended to reach to all nations in an expanded and spiritual form. It continued into the New Testament period even after the abolition of the Mosaic Covenant (Galatians 3:17). This covenant taught justification apart from works by faith alone. In contrast, the Mosaic Covenant required obedience to which the people of Israel pledged themselves (see Galatians 3:12; Exodus 19:3–6) – a promise that they did not keep. Unlike the covenant with Abraham, the Mosaic Covenant was never intended to justify anyone. These are two different covenants as to their time and place, but also as to their nature and purpose. The Mosaic Covenant's aim was to demonstrate the sinfulness of man ("Now law came in as an addition to make the trespass abound:" Romans 5:20. See also Galatians 3:19), thereby leading men to recognize their need of a Savior.

Today, Jews and Gentiles, indiscriminately, are blessed with Abraham through faith like his (Galatians 3:9). Because it has never been withdrawn and is now of universal application to all that trust in Christ, the Abrahamic Covenant is still in effect. In the Scriptures, the Abrahamic Covenant is contrasted with the Mosaic Covenant just as the latter is contrasted with the New Covenant. That, of course, is because of the fact that the Abrahamic Covenant and the New Covenant are actually two phases of one and the same covenant. All who believe in the Messiah – whether Jew or Greek – are included in it. Indeed, the fusing of the two has created a new spiritual nation, the new Israel of God (Galatians 6:16). But what is true of the Abrahamic Covenant was certainly not true of the Mosaic Covenant made at Horeb. The latter was decidedly limited in both *scope* and *duration*. That is to say, both in what it could accomplish and how long it was to last. Paul explained it this way:

> ...the law became our guardian *until* Christ came, that we might be justified by faith. But *now* that the faith has come we are *no longer under* a guardian...And if you are of Christ, then you are Abraham's seed, heirs in keeping with the promise.
>
> Galatians 3:24, 25, 29; emphasis mine

Paul unmistakably held that the Mosaic law ended with the advent of Jesus Christ. His words are unambiguous: "we are no longer under a guardian." But, in contrast, we [members of the New Covenant church] are Abraham's heirs by faith and belong to that enduring covenant.

Many years passed from the establishment of the covenant of promise to the institution of the Mosaic Covenant. During that time no compilation of laws (like the Ten Words) existed. Believing Jews who were under the Abrahamic Covenant were later admitted to the Mosaic Covenant (as well as converts like Rahab and Ruth) who by faith became participants in both covenants. But, when Christ came, the temporary covenant had run its course. The word used to describe its cessation in Hebrews 7:18 is a legal term that means "declare void, abrogate." Today, Christians are children and heirs of Abraham. But they are never said to be heirs of the Mosaic Covenant (cf. Galatians 3:12–14).

A New Covenant

Because they participate in the Abrahamic Covenant, members of the church (Jew and Gentile alike) are in the New Covenant (Galatians 3:14). This covenant was predicted by Jeremiah (31:31–34), and set over against the Mosaic Covenant as "new." According to Hebrews 8 through 10, it is also described as a "better covenant," one that was formally instituted by the Lord at the Last Supper (Matthew 26:28). The Mosaic Covenant (the "guardian") was superseded by the New Covenant when the former covenant's work was complete and no longer needed. The guardian was dismissed when the son came into manhood. As the writer of Hebrews says, the Old Covenant had become "obsolete" in his day and was "ready to disappear"[1] (Hebrews 8:13). This disappearance began to take place at the cross and was formally recognized in 70 AD at the destruction of Jerusalem, an event that completely brought down the Old Testament order of things. In Hebrews 9, the author describes the Old Covenant sanctuary and its objects of worship as "disappearing." Among these – significantly – was the Ark containing the stone tablets called the "Covenant."

Now, the Abrahamic Covenant and the New Covenant are not two distinct covenants in the way that the Mosaic and the New Covenants are. The New Covenant is "new" only in contrast to the covenant at Sinai (cf. II Corinthians 3). The New Covenant is, in effect, the "old" Abrahamic Covenant modernized (by being fulfilled). It is but a new post-messianic phase of the same covenant. The first phase included the promise; the second, its fulfillment.

Now look more closely at the covenant at Sinai. As we have seen, it was temporary, extending from Moses until Christ. Its task was merely preparatory; it was designed to lead us to Christ. It could save no one. By it God governed a temporal, theocratic nation that in all its aspects was a shadow of the spiritual kingdom of Christ. When the nation of Israel had accomplished God's purposes it too was laid aside. Neither the covenant nor the nation was intended to last. When the nation was dissolved, its covenantal constitution (the Ten

---

1. The Old Covenant would formally do so at the destruction of Jerusalem that brought a full end to it. During the forty years from Pentecost to 70 AD, there was a transition period in which the message of the New Covenant was spread throughout the then-known world (Colossians 1:6).

Words) was dissolved along with it. A new nation (spiritual Israel), together with a New Covenant constitution, superseded it (see I Peter 2:9, 10; Romans 15:12; and Matthew 21:42).

They Were the Covenant

The Ten Commandments were so essential to the Mosaic Covenant that there was no way that the covenant could be dissolved without the dissolution of Ten Words. They were, indeed, the constitution or founding document of the temporal theocracy. The Ten Commandments – as codified in Exodus and Deuteronomy – were not for all men. Nowhere does God teach them to anyone but Israel. Nor does He make it the duty of Israel or the Church to teach them. They are applicable only to Jews under the theocracy. Their *form* was strictly Jewish. However, the core, the inner intention behind them, is not. It is universal.

That the decalog *itself* was the Old Covenant[1] has not been sufficiently stressed by the Church. Yet there are unequivocal statements to that effect:

1. "And he wrote on the tablets the words of the covenant, the Ten Commandments" (Exodus 34:28);

2. "So He declared to you His covenant...that is the Ten Commandments" (Deuteronomy 4:13);

3. "And the two tablets of the covenant were in my hands" (Deuteronomy 9:15);

4. "And there I have set a place for the ark, in which is the covenant of the Lord" (I Kings 8:21);

5. "And there I have set the ark, in which is the covenant of the Lord" (II Chronicles 6:11).

---

1. That is, the "Old Agreement." The word *berith*, which is translated "covenant," refers to the God-given agreement (or arrangement) into which Israel entered. Thereby, a relationship of God-as-their-God and Israel-as-His-people was established. Throughout the Old Covenant Scriptures the covenant slogan, "I am your God and you are My people," is repeated.

In these verses the Ten Commandments themselves are said to constitute God's covenant. The tables on which the commandments were written were placed in the ark, which was then known as the "the ark of the covenant" and "the ark of the testimony." They were a testimony to the concurrence of the people with the terms of the covenant (Exodus 24:7; 25:16; Deuteronomy 9:11, 15). Pieters wrote, "What did they testify to? To the contract between God and Israel, just as among us a written contract testifies, or witnesses to an agreement."[1] When the ark was done away with, that signified the disappearance of the Old Covenant that was within it. Paul declares that the Old Covenant was a ministry of "death" (II Corinthians 3:7). Then, contrasting it with the promise of Jeremiah 31, he says the New Covenant gives "life." How could the former continue after the latter came? Life replaced death! Life trumps death!

The promise made by the Israelites was the covenantal agreement of a newly-formed temporal theocracy to keep the Ten Commandments (see Exodus 19:8). In Deuteronomy 5:1 through 21, the commandments are said to be the statutes and ordinances of the covenant that (as Moses himself pointed out) God did *not* make with their fathers (v. 3). Upon entering the land, the commandments were repeated – but in an altered form that made them refer even more exclusively to the Israelites (see especially v. 15). Pieters says, "The whole proceeding [at Mt. Sinai] shows that the Decalogue was an intensely and peculiarly national document, Israel's most precious treasure, the very life of the theocracy."[2] In his inimitable way, Luther goes so far as to say, "whoever...observes the sabbath (that is whoever teaches that it must be kept), he also

---

1. Albertus Pieters, *Notes on Old Testament History.* Grand Rapids: Wm. B. Eerdmans Publishing Co. (1950), p. 55. He went on to say, "The Decalogue being, as we have seen, the constitution, the very heart of the Old Covenant, it follows that when the said covenant passed away, the Decalogue passed away with it, as an authoritative legal document, *ibid.*, p. 57.
2. *Ibid.*

must let himself be circumcised and keep the whole Mosaic law."[1]

The church has made too much of the Ten Command-ments. She has given this code undue prominence in her cate-chisms and teaching. When Jesus was asked which was the greatest commandment, He did not turn to any of the Ten Words. Rather, He responded by quoting Deuteronomy 6:5. And, when he added the second great commandment to it, once again He by-passed Exodus 20 and located it in Leviticus 19:18. It is evident that Jesus didn't accord the same promi-nence to the decalog as many in the Church do today. That fact alone should give us pause.

A Puritan Emphasis

In particular, the Puritans taught us to place a heavy emphasis on the Ten Words. They too were the ones who sep-arated civil and ceremonial law from moral law, even though no such distinction can be found in the Bible itself. This three-fold division is a structure imposed from without. In the Pen-tateuch it was a regular practice to intersperse what have been called moral, civil, and ceremonial laws. And, a number of these laws contained material pertaining to two or even all three of these categories. Other than the fact that they are listed as a formal, unified code, why would we expect the Decalog to be different? As a matter of fact, it isn't. For instance, the reference in the fifth commandment to long life in the land of Canaan, as such, has nothing to do with chil-dren today.[2] But it was both a civil and moral command. On its moral side it now has much to do with an obedient life, prosperous in the things of the Lord.

The Sabbath, as a token (or sign) of the Mosaic Covenant (Deuteronomy 5:14, 15; Exodus 31:13) also has a ceremonial and civil as well as a moral side. Jesus Christ cracked open the shell so that its kernel may be seen. What is moral in these

---

1. In Conrad Bergendoff, *Luther's Works*, Vol. 40. Philadelphia: Muhlen-berg Press (1958), p. 94.
2. Except, of course, as it has to do with the heavenly Canaan.

commandments can be found elsewhere in the New Testament, and does not depend for its validity upon the Decalog.[1] The command to rest, for instance, is implied in the New Testament command to care for the temple of the Spirit (I Corinthians 6:19, 20). And, of course, Jesus' example is pertinent when He encouraged His disciples to come away from the crowds and "rest for a little while" (Mark 6:31). While rest on the seventh day is not a New Testament requirement, rest is. The moral duties inculcated by these commandments would be ours if we had only the New Testament, with no Decalog at all.

So, the codified Decalog was the very essence of the Mosaic Covenant, which contained both lasting and temporal elements, and was designed to serve as the founding document of a temporary kingdom. Because of their inseparability, the nation and document had to stand or fall together. And fall they did. The "guardian" has been dismissed from his duties.

The Ark with the Covenant is Gone

That the Mosaic Covenant is no longer in force is apparent from the disappearance of the ark. In Jeremiah 3:16 we are told that a time would come when the ark would disappear, and that the people would no longer think about it: "It will never come to mind, and no one will remember or visit it. It will never again be made." This, to a devout Jew, must have seemed unfathomable. The ark was the holiest piece of furniture in the temple. It was stationed in the most holy place, topped by twin Cherubim, and over it dwelt the Shekinah glory – the visible sign of God's presence. Of what time was Jeremiah speaking? When would the ark become outmoded? According to the next verse (v. 17), it would be a time when

---

1. Compare 1) Exodus 20:3 with Acts 14:15; 2) Exodus 20:4–6 with I John 5:21; 3) Exodus 20:7 with James 5:12; 5) Exodus 20:12 with Ephesians 6:2–3; 6) Exodus 20:13 with I Peter 4:16; 7) Exodus 20:14 with I Corinthians 6:9,10; 8) Exodus 20:15 with Ephesians 4:28; 9) Exodus 20:16 with Colossians 3:9; 10) Exodus 20:17 with Ephesians 5:5, I Corinthians 6:10.

"all nations (Gentiles) will be gathered to...Jerusalem." In a typical way, the New Testament church is portrayed as coming to Jerusalem, from where the Gospel emanated. Cowles says, "The ark, and surely all else with it belonging to the external forms and ceremonies of Judaism will pass away, being superseded by what is altogether better and glorious. Even the best things in that ancient system will be thought of no more."[1] That at this time the nations gather to Jehovah, not only places fulfillment of the prophecy in our era, but it seems plain as well that the doing away with the ark *of the covenant* signified the abolishment of the Mosaic Covenant which was to be replaced by the New Covenant that Jeremiah predicted (Jeremiah 31:31–33). The New Covenant, it is distinctly said, will be "not according to the covenant that I made with their fathers in the day...that I took them by the hand to bring them out of the land of Egypt" (Jeremiah 31:32). That accords with the disappearance of the ark and what it symbolized for Israel. The old was replaced by a spiritual covenant (Jeremiah 31:31–33; II Corinthians 3:1–18) that envisioned spiritual worship (John 4:21–24) carried on apart from ceremonies and symbols. The ark was last seen when the sky was opened and it was revealed to be in the heavenly temple (Revelation 11:19).

This symbolic disclosure, followed by the prophecy of the destruction of Jerusalem and the subsequent inception of Christ's reign, indicates that the earthly ark – together with the covenant it contained – by that destruction has taken on a spiritual, heavenly meaning. The earthly and temporal has given way to the heavenly and eternal. In Revelation 21:22, for instance, we read that God and His Son *are* the new temple! The heavenly rest of Hebrews 4 fits perfectly with this spiritual understanding regarding the ark.[2] The testimonial

---

1. Henry Cowles, *Jeremiah and his Lamentations; with Notes*. New York: D. Appleton & Co. (1887), p. 44.
2. For information on the interpretation of Revelation, see my book, *The Time is at Hand*.

document is no longer needed, since the nation founded upon it has ceased to exist.

Just as there was a sign attached to the first phase of the Abrahamic Covenant (circumcision) that set apart those who were under that covenant, so too the Mosaic Covenant had a sign attached to it. That sign, according to Exodus 31:13, 16 was the Sabbath[1] (see also Ezekiel 20:19, 20). The New Covenant sign, of course, is baptism. Hebrews teaches that the word "new"[2] in the New Covenant implies the abolishment of what went before (Hebrews 8:13). The "old" Mosaic Covenant – together with its "old" sign – has passed away. Baptism has replaced the Sabbath sign. In the days before Christ the Sabbath was "added' to the sign of circumcision. But in Christ all has found its fulfillment; and such shadows have given way to light. Jesus is the "body" whose shadow was cast in the form of the Old Covenant, as we have seen (Colossians 2:17). That is why, in debate, Justin Martyr told the Jew Trypho, "For the law promulgated on Horeb is now old, and belongs to yourselves [Jews] alone."[3]

In his book, *Gospel and Law*, C.H. Dodd pulls together from the epistles the teachings that new converts to Christianity received. In this interesting study it is of note that among the many varied items listed, there can be found neither instructions regarding the Ten Commandments nor even the command to keep the Sabbath. Surely, if these matters had the major significance attributed to them by modern Sabbatarians, then Gentile converts, who would not be familiar with Jewish Sabbath customs, would need careful instruction about them. But all such instruction is missing – another fatal omission! Instead, what you find is warnings about Judaizers who sought to get Gentile converts to keep "days."

---

1. Notice, the Mosaic covenantal sign was between God and Israel; no others are mentioned.

2. The word "new" is used in contrast to the Mosaic Covenant, not the Abrahamic Covenant, which was never abolished.

3. Justin Martyr, *The Apostolic Fathers, Vol 1*. Eerdmans: Grand Rapids (1987), p. 200.

A Very Serious Matter

We conclude this chapter, then, with a reminder of the words of the apostle Paul, who in sorrow and concern said of the Galatian Christians, "You are keeping days and months and years – I am afraid I have labored among you in vain" (Galatians 4:10, 11).[1] Would he say something similar to those today who claim that Sunday is the *Christian* Sabbath? Commenting on the Mosaic system in contrast to what we now enjoy in Christ, Henry Cowles wrote,

> Finally, the old system and the new have too many points of dissimilarity, not to say antagonism, to admit of being amalgamated, or in any way compounded together. The genius of the old was restrictive, exclusive, and put itself on the defensive.[2] The genius of the new is expansive, aggressive, framed to grasp the whole world.[3]

That is an insightful contrast that we might do well to consider. Isn't the matter serious enough for us to give *full* and *careful* consideration?

---

1. In his *Epistle to the Galatians* (Peabody: Hendrickson, 1987), p. 171, J.B. Lightfoot says, "the days occurring weekly are the 'sabbaths,' the monthly celebrations are the new moons, the seasons are the Passover, Pentecost, etc., and the sacred years are the sabbatical year and the year of Jubilee." This listing of four categories makes it impossible to count "days" as anything other than the weekly sabbaths.
2. Ceremonies and regulations of the Mosaic law were designed to separate the nation of Israel from other nations. Today, Jesus reigns as King of Kings and Lord of lords. His kingdom is aggressively proclaimed to all alike.
3. *Ezekiel and Daniel with Notes.* D. Appleton and Co.: New York (1890), p. 269.

CHAPTER SIX

The Ark of the Testimony

In discussions of this sort there is little or no reference to the designation "The Ark of the Testimony." Yet, it seems impossible to avoid it since the reference has to do with the Ten Commandments. According to Scriptural usage, the word "Testimony" in the designation refers specifically to these commandments which, inscribed on two tables of stone, were placed in the Ark that was fashioned as a container in which they were to be preserved. Here is what is said:

> You shall put the mercy seat on top of the ark, and in the ark you shall put the testimony which I shall give to you.   Exodus 25:21

> And when He had finished speaking with him upon Mount Sinai, He gave Moses the two tablets of the testimony, tablets of stone, written by the finger of God.   Exodus 31:18

The commandments, written on tablets of stone, are clearly designated "the testimony" and the "tablets of the testimony." These two designations undoubtedly mean that the Ten Commandments, in some sense, witnessed to something that they represented. They were not merely a summary of the moral law. They witnessed to God's covenant that the people entered into at Sinai. This can hardly be doubted.

The Commandments, as a code by which the people were to live, had a specific reference to the people of Israel who, at Sinai, were constituted a nation under God – God's people. This is said in plain words in Exodus 19:5:

> Now, then, if you will indeed obey My voice and keep My covenant, then you shall be My own possession among all the peoples, for the earth is Mine.

Exactly what God meant by that is explained in the following verse: "and you shall be to Me a kingdom of priests and a holy nation." Note that it was at this point that, by the covenant at Sinai, God constituted Israel as a "holy nation." This momentous event was to be memorialized. The ark of the testimony served that purpose. That there might be no doubt about what God and the people had covenanted to do the two tables laid up in the ark bore witness to the facts. God set forth the terms of the covenant, and the people assented: "All the people answered together and said, 'All that the Lord has spoken we will do!'" (Exodus 19:8). The ark was a witness not only to God's promises but also to the people's adherence to the terms of the covenant.

The word for "testimony" employed by Moses was *edhuth*. This Hebrew term means "to say again and again, to affirm or to prove." All three concepts were true of the testimony. Its perpetual presence said over and over again that God and His people had entered into covenant upon the terms of the Ten Commandments. They affirmed that the covenant had been made, and offered proof of the fact. That this transaction took place is unique in the Scriptures. There is no parallel to it either in the covenant made with Abraham or in the New Covenant phase of the Abrahamic Covenant. It decidedly had to do with Israel. Neither before nor after has any such testimony been laid down. It had to do with Israel alone. And, as such, the commandments (the testimony) had to do peculiarly with them. Because it stands alone, as a constitution for the Jews, it is not for us. There should be no doubt, then, that the Decalog was treated in a way that was unique to Israel.

A testimony is that which gives assurance of the truth of something else. The isolation of the Ten Commandments in their unique form (no other laws were written by God's finger) and their insertion into the ark, were to assure all concerned that the covenant was made *on the basis of adherence to these commandments*. The testimony was not to some moral law that was to be distinguished from the other commandments. In what way would doing so constitute them as a "testimony?" To what would they "testify?" But, to understand them as the foundational covenant of the new nation that the people of God were to remember makes sense. The Sinaitic covenant was, in *essence*, the Ten Commandments:

> So He declared to you His covenant which he commanded you to perform, that is, the Ten Commandments; and He wrote them on two tablets of stone.   Deuteronomy 4:13

Again, that the covenant was made uniquely with Israel is affirmed in Deuteronomy 5:2, 3:

> The Lord our God made a covenant with us at Horeb. The Lord did not make this covenant with our fathers, but with us, with all those of us alive here today.

So, the Ark of the Testimony is the box containing the covenantal requirements to which Israel assented so as to become a nation. It is called such because it gave testimony to the fact.

CHAPTER SEVEN

What was Abolished?

We must examine Ephesians 2:15 where Paul says that Jesus made peace between Jew and Gentile believers "by *abolishing* in His flesh the law of commandments with its *regulations*" (emphasis mine). To do justice to our study it is impossible to bypass these words. They refer to something in the old order that was "abolished." What was it?

Consider Paul's Terminology

First, take a look at the verb in the phrase. It is *katargeo*, a Greek word that carries the meanings of "abolish, annul, make of no effect, abrogate." It is appropriate for describing something of which the force has been eliminated. Every one of these possible translations points to commandments that were done away with at the completion of the work of Jesus Christ on the cross. There is no question, then, about two facts:

1. Something was revoked because of Christ's death;
2. That which was revoked was "the law of commandments with its regulations."

Now, we must come to an understanding of what the words "law," "commandments," and regulations" mean in this context.

Also, it will be necessary to understand the genitive "of." There seems to be only one way in which to take it: "the law, which *consists of* commandments." All other interpretations seem far-fetched or present insuperable difficulties. So, then, we are talking about an Old Testament Law that consisted of commandments which, by various subordinate decrees, regulated the lives of the Israelites.[1]

---

1. Perhaps Edersheim best explains the import of these words when he speaks of "thirty-nine chief classes, or 'fathers'" of work that the Jews concluded must be avoided on the Sabbath, each of which was subdivided into

Next, consider the word translated "regulations." This term has also been translated "ordinances" or "decrees." But "regulations" seems most appropriate. The Greek term is *dogma*, a word that at that time had not yet acquired the modern denotation of officially held tenets of a church or denomination. The idea behind the expression is that there were legitimate regulations that were *related to* the commandments. Paul was saying that the Law consisted of commandments that, in turn, were to be kept by observing the regulations that were required by each.

Some Conclusions

The remaining question is *what* law, having commandments and regulations, did Paul have in mind? There are but two possibilities:

1. The "law" in question refers to the entire Old Testament with all its commandments and their regulations, or

2. The "law of commandments" refers to the Ten Commandments together with the subordinate regulations for carrying them out.

Either way, the Ten Commandments are included in the designation. On the one hand, if Paul referred to the decalog, or on the other, if he subsumed it in the larger designation, the decalog is included. Either way, the Sabbath commandment is included. These commandments in the Law, and all of the regulations by which one was to observe them, then, are in view.

The Importance of the Word "Regulations"

In addition to circumcision, Sabbath Day regulations (the ways in which the fourth commandment was to be observed)

"ever so many 'descendants,' or subordinate divisions." Alfred Edersheim, *The Temple, Its Ministry and Services* (New York: Anson D.F. Randolph Co., 1874), p. 148. While these divisions were not inspired, they do illustrate Paul's point. If anything about the law exhibited what Paul referred to, it would be Sabbath regulations, *par excellence*. C. K. Barrett lists all thirty-nine "fathers" by name in his *New Testament Background: Selected Documents* (New York: The Macmillan Company, 1957), p. 154.

separated the Jews from the Gentiles. That is quite evident to every Bible student. It is not a matter of debate. Later, I will show something of the evidence for this claim. It is important not to minimize the import of Paul's words. He says that the blood of Jesus Christ made peace between believing Jew and Gentile, creating from them "one new man," who was no longer subject to the Old Testament commandments and their regulations. Abolishment of these regulations made the coming together of the two possible.

The latter point – that their regulations were abolished along with the commandments to which they were subjoined – helps us understand that the *principles* contained in the Law are still valid for us. How is that? Paul's emphasis is on the "regulations." It is that which sharply qualifies his statement about the commandments. It indicates that it was this *functional aspect* of the commandments (their regulations) that was of particular importance in creating a separation between Jew and Gentile. How the commandments functioned – their daily outward influence on others – is precisely what stood between Jew and Gentile. And that was what was done away with.[1]

That a child should honor his father and mother is a universal truth from God, as valid for Gentile as for Jew (as we see in Ephesians 6). But that rebellious children should be stoned to death (which was a regulation or requirement of the theocratic law) is not so. That people must rest is a universally recognized fact. But that they should do so by observing the Jewish seventh day Sabbath, with all of its requirements and regulations, is not. Thus we see that it is the regulations attached to the commandments, in particular, that kept Jew

---

1. See chapter sixteen for an account of how the matter of separation between Jews and Gentiles became so much of an issue in the early church that a conference had to be called to deal with it. When Paul addressed Peter, who was "living like a Gentile," but whose later behavior indicated that Gentiles should live as Jews, it was this very question of *separation* by Jewish commandments that was at issue. Keeping Jewish customs separated Jew from Gentile – as they were intended to in the previous age.

and Gentile apart. With the abrogation of the Sabbath *regulations*, the principle of rest could be retained in a form that was compatible with a spiritual, worldwide church rather than a temporal, national theocracy. This abolition of the commandments, in their regulatory functions, brought about a new order and a new man.

The passage, as you can see, is not only valuable in helping us to understand that the law of commandments was abolished, but also in showing that it was done so by eliminating the regulations that separated Jew from Gentile. The principle behind each of the commandments remains in force today.[1] Understanding this helps us to resolve the seeming contradiction between Ephesians 2:14 and Romans 3:31. In the latter passage Paul teaches that faith *doesn't* abolish the Law. Does Paul contradict himself? Of course not! The Law, in its essence is not abolished, but the regulations by which it was enforced before the coming of Jesus Christ *were* done away with. It is these regulations that are in question, and that no longer have force.

At the coming of Jesus, God replaced the shadows of the law, that were found especially in the decrees (regulations) attached to the commandments, with the eternal reality – a spiritual, ultimate reality that, unlike the Old Covenant, would never give way to another covenantal order of things (Romans 7:6). So, in this sense, Paul could write, "we are *establishing* the law" (Romans 3:31).[2] In its inner essence, in its moral principles, the Law – both its intention and import – was established in and by Christ Himself. He is for us all that the Law sets forth (I Corinthians 1:30). The authority of the

---

1. As the French Confession of Faith (prepared by Calvin, and issued in 1559) says, "We believe that the ordinances of the law came to an end at the advent of Jesus Christ; but, although the ceremonies are no more in use, yet their substance and truth remain in the person of him in whom they are fulfilled." Philip Schaff, *The Creeds of Christendom*, Vol III. Grand Rapids: Baker Book House (1990), p. 373.

2. That is to say, setting it into its permanent, final, unchangeable form. The verb, *histano*, means "to make stand."

Law did not come from its regulations, however. Just the opposite is true. This should be clear from the way the New Testament treats these regulations. The authority of the regulations came from the inner reality behind them.

Why, then, would Christians today want to re-establish the shadowy aspects of the commandments when they now have the reality? To do so is to erect again the middle wall of partition that divided Jew from Gentile. With Luther, it is proper to say, "We will regard Moses as a teacher [there is much to learn from his writings] but we will not regard him as our lawgiver, unless he agrees with the New Testament and the natural law.[1] Therefore, it is clear enough that Moses is the lawgiver of the Jews and not of the Gentiles."[2]

---

1. By "natural law" he meant the law written on the heart (Romans 2:15).
2. In William M. Landeen, *Martin Luther's Religious Thought*. Mountain View & Omaha: Pacific Press Publishing Association (1971), p. 187.

CHAPTER EIGHT

Jesus and the Sabbath

What more is there to discuss? The answer: a good bit more. For instance, we must consider the reason why the church meets on Sunday, the first day of the week, and calls it the "Lord's Day." More must be made of rest itself, and man's need for it. In addition, we need to think about what can or cannot be done on the Lord's Day. But, before coming to these important matters, we must discuss how Jesus kept the Sabbath – and how what He did pertains to us today.

Jesus – Our Example of Sabbath-Keeping?

Many of those who promote Sabbath-keeping point to the example of Jesus: "Since Jesus kept the Sabbath, we should keep it." That sounds good – on the surface. But there are several things wrong with this reasoning. First, not everything that Jesus did was intended to provide an example for us. He raised Lazarus from the dead. He went up into a mountain to be transfigured. And, preeminently, He died on the cross for the sins of His people. None of these things was done to provide an example for us to take similar actions.

But, beyond that, and of greater significance for our present concern, Paul underlines the truth that Jesus was "born under law" (Galatians 4:4). That means He was subject to Old Testament law.[1] He did not live in the new era, but in the old. The regulations of the Mosaic period – including those pertaining to the Sabbath – were still in effect. He was an Old Covenant Jew. In contrast, Paul wrote

---

1. At His baptism, when He was officially anointed as the Messiah ("the Anointed One"), Jesus explained to John that it was necessary for Him to "fulfill all righteousness" (Matthew 3:15). Among other things, that meant He was subjecting Himself to everything that a pious Jew should. No Christian may submit to John's baptism as He did, because it has been superseded by Jesus' baptism (cf. Acts 19:1–7). Once again, we must understand that the new has replaced the old!

that the Law was a guardian *until* Christ came, but that now that he has come "we are no longer under a guardian" (Galatians 3:24, 25). And he stoutly affirmed, "You aren't under law but under grace" (Romans 6:14).

Clearly, then, our status in relation to the Mosaic Law differs from Christ's. The dismissal of the guardian brought about an entirely different state of affairs. The son grew up. He no longer takes orders from the guardian, who has been dismissed. The change that resulted from this fact was what the Jerusalem conference was all about (Acts 15). Since Christ came and died, neither a Gentile nor a Jewish Christian is required to live according to symbolic Jewish ordinances. Indeed, as we have already seen, very little of the "burden" of the Law was carried over (Acts 15:28). The "burden" mentioned by the conferees referred to the shadowy provisions of the Mosaic order. And, when New Testament churches were tempted to observe them, Paul wrote "It was for freedom that Christ freed us; stand firm, therefore, and don't subject yourselves again to a yoke of slavery"[1] (Galatians 5:1). In saying this, he was referring not only to circumcision (which was the main question at the conference and in the book of Galatians as a whole), but to keeping the Sabbath. In view of Galatian Judaizing he also wrote, "You are keeping days and months and seasons and years – I am afraid I have labored among you in vain!" (Galatians 4:10, 11). Keeping these, according to the regulations attached to them, was a part of that yoke. Paul obviously considered the keeping of various days to be an unmistakable sign of dangerous Judaizing tendencies. These must be eliminated because Christ has truly made both Jew and Gentile one "by abolishing in His flesh the law of commandments with its regulations" (Ephesians 2:15).

---

1. In contrast to that "burden" and "yoke of slavery," Jesus urged, "Come to Me, all who labor and are heavily burdened, and I will refresh you. Put My yoke on you and learn from Me...My yoke is easy to wear and My burden is light" (Matthew 11:29, 30).

How Jesus Kept the Sabbath

Jesus refused to keep the Sabbath according to the traditions that the elders had heaped upon the fourth commandment. He healed on the Sabbath, though some of the Jews forbade it as "work." Justifying this Sabbath work, He argued that it was lawful to do good on the Sabbath. He also justified plucking grain as His disciples walked through a field of it. When the Jews found fault and pointed fingers, He declared that He was "Lord of the Sabbath" (Matthew 12:8). Jesus did not explicate that statement, but if it means anything surely it means, "Since I am the One who gave you the Sabbath, it is I, not you, Who must define its meaning and proper observance." His example, which so markedly differed from that of the Scribes and the Pharisees, *was* the proper example of true Sabbath-keeping *for an Israelite*.

In addition to His declaration that He was Lord of the Sabbath, Jesus also said that "The Sabbath was made for man's sake, not man for the Sabbath's sake" (Mark 2:27). He saw the Sabbath as a benefit to man as well as a way of glorifying God. Man's benefits were superior to the *act* of Sabbath-keeping. He gave an example of how human physical need superseded ceremonial law: when hungry, David even appropriated the "presentation loaves" (Mark 2:26). And He noted that the priests in the temple also "broke" the Sabbath (Matthew 12:3–8).

From these instances we see that He could not have considered the Sabbath so important that doing God's will in other respects could not transcend the obligation to keep it. It should be noted that in and of itself, therefore, Sabbath observance was not a moral duty. Rest was. But the act, *per se*, was not.[1] How is that so?

No moral duty may be violated for the sake of another. God never puts us in a situation where we must refuse to do one required good in order to do some other good. We never

---

1. It was a moral duty, however, insofar as by keeping it He was obeying God's law. But there was nothing more moral than that about the act.

have to disobey one requirement of God in order to obey another.

Fundamentally, the Sabbath was a sign of the Covenant that honored God and that had side-benefits for man (Exodus 31:13). It was to be observed in order to remember God's creation, Israel's deliverance, and the people's separation from the world. As a sign, it had symbolic meaning. Jesus' words indicate that David could still observe the spirit of the commandment in his heart even when failing to conform to the outward sign. Surely, the hard-hearted Pharisees, who cared more for the welfare of their sheep than for a human being, though keeping it outwardly, failed to keep the Sabbath at all.[1]

The Sabbath in 70 AD

Now, what shall we say about Jesus' words concerning flight from Jerusalem on the Sabbath? He said, "Pray that your flight won't take place in winter or on a Sabbath, because there will be great affliction ..." (for the complete picture, see Matthew 14:15–21; Luke 21:20–24). The Destruction of Jerusalem in 70 AD, to which this prophecy was directed, even in its preliminary stage was, as Jesus predicted, a terrible event. However, Titus, the Roman general in charge of the siege of the city, briefly withdrew his armies, and the Christians fled as Jesus had directed. The armies then surrounded the city once again, never to depart until it was razed – together with the temple.

Jesus mentions the haste with which Christians should flee. There would be no time to take valuables with them. To get out with their lives was enough. If a woman was pregnant that would, of course, cause difficulty in the flight. If the day of flight was on a Sabbath, that too would hinder the escape. By that last comment, Jesus did not mean that Christians would have difficulty in deciding whether or not to go (in order to keep the Sabbath). Rather, what He had in mind was encountering possible restrictions against travel as well as

---

1. Their concern, of course, was not for the sheep, but to avoid financial loss (see Matthew 12:11).

danger in traveling over a battlefield. The Jews had a rule that one should not go beyond a Sabbath day's journey – which was far less than a trip to the distant mountains to which Jesus directed them. That the gates of the city would be closed on the Sabbath, is one example of a problem that might arise. The emphasis in the prophecy is entirely upon difficulties that might be encountered when fleeing in haste. To take His words to mean that it would be breaking the Sabbath to flee on that day is to read into the prophecy ideas for which there is no justification.

So, we learn some important facts about Sabbath-keeping from what Jesus said about it. Obviously, He refused to keep the traditions of the elders and even showed considerable flexibility in His understanding of how the day should be kept. His approach was quite different from the rigid manner in which some today, who wish to impose a near-Judaistic Sabbath on the church, insist that it must be observed. In that He focused on the inner intent of the law, Jesus *is* our Example!

If, indeed, the Sabbath was symbolic, as we saw, we must now examine the "rest" that it symbolized more fully. That is what we shall do in the next chapter.

CHAPTER NINE

Rest from Labor among the Thorns

Certainly, as we saw in chapter six, there is a moral as well as a shadowy ceremonial aspect to the fourth commandment. The need for rest remains even though the old requirements have disappeared. Just as we apply the element in the fifth commandment having to do with the land of Canaan to something else,[1] we must treat similar aspects of the Sabbath similarly. Among other things, the Sabbath memorializes God's rest at Creation. He rested after completing His work. Of course, God wasn't tired; the rest pointed to the completion of His creative activity to His own satisfaction (Genesis 1:31).

Because of the sinful bent of the nature received from Adam, man tends to forget. In addition to its sign value, then, the Sabbath also helped Israel to "remember" (Deuteronomy 15). As we learn from the Old Testament accounts of God's dealings with Israel, they were a people with a great propensity to forget! He knew that they would need a visible, weekly reminder. Sadly, they failed to use the Sabbath that He provided for that purpose. Instead, they hardened their hearts against it. They turned God's gracious provision into a mere ceremony, and quickly forgot the reality behind it. This tendency is seen in their failure to understand the types and shadows of the law. As a ceremony, Sabbath keeping became the center of attention, rather than God, Whose praise and honor were to be called for by it. Thus, it wasn't long before they became legalists, rigidly focusing on external man-made rules and regulations. This problem continued until the time of Christ.[2]

But what of the value of rest to human beings? In the garden episode God cursed the ground because of Adam's sin. The

---

1. Usually, to a long and peaceful life among God's people (as evidenced in Hebrews 12:22–24).
2. It is clear from the New Testament that, at the time when Christ came, there was a remnantof faithful Jews who understood the inner meaning of the Law. But they were the exception, not the rule.

curse turned the blessings of work into toil and labor. Now man must eat by the sweat of his brow, laboring against the thorns and weeds that sprang up to choke out the plants. And he would, in the end, return to the dust (Genesis 3:17–19). This terrible curse, in effect, was a curse upon all labor. It was not intended to be limited to agriculture (which was only illustrative of how it would work). Because Adam's prime function was to cultivate and protect a pleasant and fruitful garden, the curse was given in terms of that setting. But everyone who labors, whether in a factory at a machine, in an office seated at a computer, or at home keeping house, also experiences the problems now connected with work. Machinery breaks down and must be fixed, discarded or replaced; the office is filled with workers who are not immune to mistakes, misunderstandings, sloth, rivalry and malice, and the home knows wear and tear not only on the carpets but also on the spirits of its occupants. Everyone fights against the "thorns"! From time to time, therefore, there is need to refresh oneself. Believers are not exempt from this need; they too must get away from the "grind" of the curse to find the rejuvenation that is found in resting. Otherwise, they will forget God and find themselves entangled in the thorns.

In addition to its sign value, the Sabbath was to be a physical blessing to the Israelites and those who worked for them: "the Sabbath was made for man." They were given a "day off" in which to recuperate and contemplate God and His works.[1] Instead of appreciating and encouraging such a use of the Sabbath, the elders turned it into a burden rather than a delight. Symbolism and refreshment alike were submerged under the swell of rules and regulations. The sheer weight of the Pharisaical "Sabbath Police System" added to the burden. But, in spite of all of this, the moral aspect of the commandment remains. It is beneficial in every age. The Christian, for instance, recog-

---

1. O. Palmer Robertson put it well: "The Old Testament saints were looking forward to the coming rest from the burden of sin, just as each week they looked forward to their rest from work on the Sabbath Day." In *New Horizons Magazine*, Vol. 24, No. 3, March 2003, p. 5.

nizes the need for rest to keep the temple of the Holy Spirit functioning well so as to honor and serve God (see I Corinthians 6:19, 20).

One Day in Seven?

But is a *seventh day* cessation of work mandatory? Must the believer stop work one day out of seven? Is he bound to a strict, every-week routine, and failure to keep it constitutes grievous sin? Could there be times when circumstances call for doubling up work, to be followed by doubled up periods of rest? If he travels in his work, must he stop on Sunday to be sure that by his travel he doesn't cause pilots, flight attendants, and others to work? But if he interrupts his travel, he then causes others who cook meals and care for the activities that go on in motels to work! He seems caught in the mesh of it all. Must he also consider whether or not he may "light fires" in a northern climate when the temperature is below freezing? May he turn up the thermostat, or must he avoid doing so because workers at the generating plant must watch over the electrical units that supply his house?[1] Is he to lobby for one day and night set aside by the government for everyone – believers and unbelievers alike – to observe a period of rest? May people take their rest periods on different days, if – like hospital workers – they must work on Sunday?[2] The answer to these, and a host of similar questions, is that God has not decreed that Christians keep the Sabbath day. All other answers lead to hopeless casuistry. We do not have to trouble our minds about such matters. Remember, Paul speaks out against the keeping of days.

---

1. Or, to be entirely consistent, shouldn't he turn it off the night before? May he "buy" electricity on the Sabbath?
2. Not everyone is involved in works of "mercy" as hospital workers are. But where is the dividing line? Is it a work of mercy to serve people in restaurants who might have eaten at home? Or who might have postponed a trip until later in the week? And if a Christian must travel on Sunday in order to keep his job, are the financial considerations involved to be considered "mercy" toward his family? On and on we might go, but I'll spare you the agony.

Christians in Other Times

It is convenient for many Americans to have Sunday off from work so that they may attend church services. But not everyone has such privileges. The early church faced the problem of finding a time to meet. The state didn't provide for it as it does in our land. That made the "assembling of themselves together" difficult. Early records tell us that the churches gathered well before dawn in order to be able to meet together. Pliny (a pagan official) writing to the governor Trajan said that Christians were "in the habit of meeting on a certain fixed day before it was light."[1] Doubtless, Christian slaves and other workers assembled before the day began because they would be required to go to work later in the day. Probably for the same reason, Paul preached in Troas at night (Acts 20:7). We, who find it much easier to attend church, probably appreciate church services less. Would Christian community worship mean more if we had to arise before daylight to enjoy it?

We must conclude that there is no requirement for Christians to set aside any specific day for worship, service, and rest. That they are to do all three is true because other passages of Scripture mandate it. But even meeting on the first day of the week is not a scriptural command. Moreover, the modern teaching that the Sabbath was changed to a one-day-in-seven Lord's Day cannot be found in the Bible. Search as you may, you won't find any such thing. The conclusions that these facts demand are two:

1. Every Christian must rest his body and mind in order to glorify God by them.

2. Every Christian must assemble together with other believers for worship at a time most convenient for all.[2]

---

1. *Pliny to Trajan,* X: 96 in the Loeb Classical Library, Vol. II, p. 402.
2. The elders must determine what time is best for the benefit of all the members of the body. Preferably, they should meet on the Lord's Day – as we shall see.

CHAPTER TEN

Sign Language

As we have seen, unlike the other nine commandments, the Sabbath is called a "sign." In Ezekiel 20:12 we read, "Also I gave them My Sabbaths to be a *sign* between Me and them, that they might know that I am the Lord who sanctifies them." And in the same chapter, verse 20 reads, "Sanctify My Sabbaths, and they shall be a *sign* between Me and you that you may know that I am the Lord your God." That unique feature of the fourth commandment, as well as the special yearly Sabbaths, sharply distinguished Jews from the others. The Sabbath sign designated them as God's people.

A sign is not the thing signified. A sign reading HOUSE FOR SALE is not the sale itself. The rainbow in the clouds was a sign of God's promise (Genesis 9:11–13, 17), but it was not the promise which it was to bring to mind every time it occurred. In a bold anthropomorphism, God said that the covenantal rainbow sign would help Him to remember His promise (v. 16). Of course, unlike us, God never forgets.

Now the Sabbath, likewise, was given to help God's people "know" that God was their God. This fact is stressed in the two passages above. Similarly, in the two places where the Sabbath law is set forth (Exodus 20:8–11; Deuteronomy 5:12–15), the day is called a sign designed to help His people "remember." The two concepts converge: man is a forgetful creature; God gave him a sign to help him remember. Keeping the Sabbath day holy (special) was intended to give man *opportunity* to pause and remember. He was to remember how God created the world, how He chose Israel to be His people and how there would be ultimate rest in the heavenly Canaan. Remembering would help him to know and love God.[1]

---

1. Some have attempted to explain the word "remember" *strictly* as an exhortation to remember the past (either in creation or elsewhere). Obeying the command to remember (observe) the day *was* to help Jews remem-

But keeping the day holy, that is, "set apart" from other days, was not the same as remembering or knowing. This is clear from the many instances in which the Jews "kept" the day, but forgot its significance. Indeed, the Pharisees even *added* rules to the simple commandment requirements in order to assure that they *would* keep it "holy." These turned out to be one reason they failed to remember or know what it signified. Unlike the covenantal sign given to Noah, which was perpetual, and could not be made otherwise, the Sabbath sign was attached to a temporary covenant. The code of commandments was meant for the time when the people were living "in the land" (Deuteronomy 4:14). Moreover, the Sabbath sign differed from the rainbow in that faithful observance of the sign depended on man, not upon God.

In that the fourth commandment has sign value, it differs from the rest of the commandments in the code. Remember, a sign points to something other than itself. The Sabbath, like the Lord's Supper, also was a help to the Jews to "remember." In the Lord's Supper, Jesus' death for our sins is remembered by its proper observance. Yet, people often "observe" the sacrament unworthily, not discerning the Lord's body (I Corinthians 11:29). That is to say, they miss the intent of the sacrament – they fail to employ it properly for their own benefit and the Lord's honor. The same potential problem occurs with any sign or symbol.

The other nine commandments are unlike the fourth in that they are not one step removed from the thing itself. When one commits adultery (either physically or spiritually) he has thereby engaged in the forbidden act. The seventh commandment isn't a sign of something else; it is the outright

---

ber the past. But, when viewed as a command to observe it, as Oehler rightly says, "'Remember' is not intended to recall the Sabbath to mind as an ancient *institution*, but requires the people to be from that time onward mindful of the Sabbath-day, and thus entirely corresponds with the 'observe' of the parallel passage, Deuteronomy 5:12'" (emphasis mine). Gustav Friedrich Oehler, *Theology of the Old Testament*. Grand Rapids: Zondervan Pub. House (n.d.), p. 328.

prohibition of the act (in heart or body). The same is true of the eight others. In some ways, however, Sabbath-keeping is akin to circumcision, which also was a sign. Again, in circumcision, one may perform the act without understanding its significance. It was a sign and seal of the righteousness that comes by faith (Romans 4:9–11).[1] But all too often this significance was lost: zealous to circumcise their children and proselytes, the Jews failed to recognize its meaning. One was just as likely to miss the sign value of Sabbath-keeping while (outwardly) observing it differently from other days of the week.

The early church had problems with those who carried over the sign of circumcision into the new era, and a conference had to be held to adjudicate the matter (Acts 15). In dealing with Judaizing teachings that were adversely affecting the churches in Galatia, Paul went so far as to say, "In Christ Jesus neither circumcision nor uncircumcision is of any account, but only faith working through love" (Galatians 5:6; see also 6:12–15). Its observance, *for its own sake,* rather than for its intent, motivated these Judaizers. The same can be true of those who show such zeal for keeping the Sabbath today. How frequently do you hear them *recalling* the creation rest, the rest from slavery in Egypt,[2] the sanctifying of the people of God, and speaking in *anticipation* of the eternal rest?

In his Gospel, when John used the word "sign" to refer to Christ's authenticating miracles, he did not mention the two other terms that are also applied to miracles: "powers" (usually translated "miracles") and "wonders." They speak respectively of the event itself and its effect upon those who witnessed it. The word "sign" refers to the design or purpose of the event. That was John's sole concern. In and of themselves these important events were meaningless. People witnessed an extraordinary event and were astonished at it. But what was its purpose? Why did it happen? John pointed to

---

1. There was a negative side to the sign which Paul mentions in Colossians 2:11: it is a picture of the "putting off of the body of flesh."
2. Of course, to remember the exodus as something that pertains to liberating Christians (except in a spiritual sense) makes no sense.

signs for their evidentiary value – that men may know and believe that Jesus is the promised Messianic Redeemer, to the salvation of their souls (John 20:30, 31). That was the *value* of the signs. He wanted "customers" to buy, not to focus on the sign on the front of the house! God expected the same of Sabbath-keepers.

So, the question comes down to this: is keeping the sign the same as observing that which it signifies?[1] The answer, as the Scriptures repeatedly make clear, is, "No." It most emphatically is not. Well, then, do we still need the Sabbath to help us to remember creation rest and rest from Egyptian slavery? To remind us that Israel was God's people? No such emphasis is found in the New Testament. Rather, in Hebrews 4 the eternal rest comes vividly into view. Even the faithful Patriarchs, who lived in the land of Palestine, looked beyond Canaan to the eternal rest in the heavenly city (Hebrews 11:13–16, 39, 40). That means they understood that the promise of the land of Canaan was but a sign of the eternal land and city of God. Together with them we should look forward, not backward. But even looking backward should serve only to stimulate thought about "something better" that is "in sight" (v. 40).

---

1. Signs were attached to covenants. The rainbow was a sign of the Noahic covenant, circumcision of the Abrahamic Covenant, the Sabbath of the Mosaic Covenant, and baptism of the New Covenant.

CHAPTER ELEVEN

The Change of Symbolism

The interesting thing about the fourth commandment is that we do not know exactly what it is. What?" you say. That's right. It's given in one form in Exodus 20:8–11 but in another form in Deuteronomy 5:12–15. The fact is that the wording in Deuteronomy differs from that in Exodus. Doubtless, this is because the second writing was more appropriate to the changed conditions when it was given. But, of course, both required a Sabbath rest on the seventh day. However, when it comes to the *reason* given for doing so, there is a significant difference. We cannot, therefore, simply speak of *the* fourth commandment. In the code, there are two.[1]

In Exodus, the reason mentioned for remembering to keep the Sabbath Day holy is to help Jews to recall the creative activity of God that was completed in six days. God then "rested" on the seventh day – not because He was tired (as we noted), but because He wanted the day to remind the Israelites that He is their Creator.[2] The reason for keeping the Sabbath that is found in Deuteronomy, however, is to help them remember the difficult days in Egypt from which He delivered them. And, while we are at it, we might mention those passages in Ezekiel in which a third reason is given: "I also gave them My sabbaths to be a sign between Me and them, that they might know that I am the Lord who sanctifies them (Ezekiel 20:12; see also v. 20). Here, the Sabbath was to become a sign of the special relationship of God to His people

---

1. Once again, the fourth commandment stands out as unique.
2. That the Ten Commandments were not for all men generally, seems clear. Nowhere does God teach them to anyone but Israel. Nor does He make it the duty of Israel or the Church to do so. And he does not hold Gentiles accountable for breaking the fourth commandment. While of universal moral value, their form – and what it required – made the commandment appropriate only to the Jews. No other people was delivered from Egypt.

A third reading? Why the changes? Why must the Sabbath change its meaning and purpose again and again?

To the command in Exodus, Moses affixed the thought that bodily rest symbolizing the cessation of God's creative activity ought to lead to rest from toil and labor under the curse. The explanation is rather straightforward. But in the Deuteronomy entry he mentioned the Egyptian deliverance. And to Ezekiel, God Himself – not mentioning creation or Egypt – said that the sign "sanctified" Israel. That is to say, it "set them apart" to Him and from other peoples. Rest remains – but the reason for it changes.

The Changes are Significant

What is the importance of these changes? Well, it is note-worthy that through time the Sabbath has been viewed differently in different contexts. And, in each instance, the change was God's doing, not man's. Obviously, then, there was no rigid, monolithic statute as many conceive of it. It has had sign-value of different sorts. That means that it *is not unchangeable*. Indeed, it is the one commandment of the Ten that is changeable. The idea of rest was used in various contexts to emphasize different things. Israel's rest has always been in view, as has the idea of rest *per se*, but God preeminently is the concern: God's creative activity, God's redemptive activity and God's theocratic rule of Israel. The first two reasons, that God rested on the Seventh day and that He brought His people out of Egypt, focus on the past. The third, that they would know He is the Lord who sanctifies them, on the writer's (Ezekiel's) present. In these changes, there seems to be a temporal progression as each reason gives way to the next. Is it unreasonable to expect that since the great change of the Old to the New Testament era, there would be a fourth – *future* reason? It would seem almost certain that this would happen. The symbolism seems attached to the changing conditions of God's people in relationship to God.

The nation of Israel, as God's political, theocratic state, passed away with the coming of Jesus Christ. Instead, God took to Himself a new nation, a people that had not previously been a people (I Peter 2:10). This new, worldwide kingdom today is *spiritual* Israel, God's present "people" (I Peter 2:9, 10). With the passing of the former nation of Israel as God's special people, the need for Israel's redemptive and theocratic signs also passed. A spiritual symbolism for a spiritual people came into being.

Remember Hebrews Four

That a fourth reason is given in Hebrews four can hardly be contested. The Sabbath now pictures the heavenly rest – the final Sabbath. It is the culmination of all that went before. Of it, all the others were but types and shadows. This is the ultimate New Testament concept of rest. In contrast to the others, it focuses upon the future of the eternal state of all the covenant people of God (Hebrews 4:11). The symbolism is in keeping with the New Covenant that is written on the heart rather than on tables of stone (II Corinthians 3:3). It is spiritual rest into which one enters upon his death or at the coming of Christ – not physical rest in this life on earth. In part, however, Christians have already "tasted" something of "the world to come" (Hebrews 6:4), and in their hearts and minds have come to the heavenly Jerusalem (Hebrews 12:18ff.). As there are no more sacrifices and no more temple service because Jesus is the reality that these things symbolized, so too Paul says, there is no more Sabbath, because the "rest-reality" is found in Christ – now in part and forever in the end. This eternal rest is permanent, never to give way to another change. The eternal Sabbath is the sign of our everlasting rest in Christ.

Paul, who underwent serious difficulties of various sorts, nevertheless was able to fulfil his ministry because he looked forward to this reality (II Corinthians 4:8; 6:4; 11:21ff.). Looking for the thornless day, he worked successfully against the thorns of this life. He called that heavenly rest "an eternal weight of glory" (II Corinthians 4:17). He said, "The Lord... will save me for His heavenly kingdom. To Him be glory forever and ever!" (II Timothy 4:18). Looking ahead – rather than behind – made all the difference! In Revelation 14:13, looking ahead to the martyrs who would give their lives for Christ – of which Paul was one – John wrote, "Happy are the dead who die in the Lord from now on...they may rest from their toil; their works follow them." The word "toil" is *kopos*, which refers to troublesome labor and fatigue – in short, work against the thorns. This *forward* look is what should motivate us today.

As we worship, neither in Jerusalem nor on Mt. Gerazim, but in Spirit and in truth, we worship, wherever we may be, out of the measure of spiritual rest that we have already found in Jesus.[1] In summing up Calvin's view of the Sabbath commandment, Jonathan Edwards wrote, "And if [the fourth commandment] stands in force now only signifying a spiritual rest,...it doth not remain as one of the ten commandments, but as a summary of all the commands."[2] Now, that is a thought worth pondering!

It is a commandment that differs from the rest – none of which was a sign, and none of which was changed from time to time. That it is called a sign ought to alert us to its uniqueness and, therefore, that it should be treated differently. At last, the Sabbath has emerged from among the shadows. Its new, eternal, ultimate sign value is for *us* today. We must not minimize the commandment, but we must move from thinking of it in its temporal, theocratic sense.

---

1. The Heidelberg Catechism captures this well: "...all the days of my life I cease from my evil works, and yield myself to the Lord, to work by His Holy Spirit in me: and thus begin in this life the eternal sabbath" (Lord's Day 38).
2. In Richard Gaffin, *Calvin and the Sabbath* (Fearn, Ross-shire: Mentor, 1998), p. 145.

CHAPTER TWELVE

The First Day – A Sabbath?

Christians assembled on the first day from the beginning. Everyone who studies the Sabbath question knows the arguments for keeping the first day of the week. The Bible speaks of meetings on the first day, of celebrating the agape feasts on the first day, and laying aside money for the poor on the first day. I won't even bother to discuss these verses that refer to these practices since the knowledge of these facts is universal. And it is well-known why the church chose this day: to commemorate the resurrection of Jesus. These facts are not in dispute except by Seventh Day Baptists and Seventh Day Adventists, whose torturous arguments I will not waste your time to discuss.

Now, not so commonly known, though all biblical scholars are well aware of them, are the writings from the early church that confirm the following facts:

1. The church met on the first day of the week, also known as the Lord's Day (cf. Revelation 1:10).

2. The church explained that the Lord's Day memorializes the resurrection.

3. The church decided to worship early in the morning.

4. For a time, some celebrated both the Jewish Sabbath *and* the Christian Lord's Day.

These facts are incontrovertible and unchallenged.

The First Day Not a Sabbath

There is one fact that is striking because of its omission from *all* of the early accounts: none of them treats the first day as a Sabbath.[1] None of them speaks of the Sabbath as hav-

---

1. Philip Schaff says, "The fathers did not regard the Christian Sunday as a continuation of, but a substitute for, the Jewish Sabbath...the ante-Nicene church clearly distinguished the Christian Sunday from the Jewish Sabbath, and put it on an independent ground." By this, he meant that they did not

ing been changed from Saturday to Sunday. Indeed, the absence of any such thing in all of these accounts is not only suspicious, it is telling. If it were true that the Sabbath day, with its rules and regulations, had been changed, here was the place to discover the fact. But it just isn't there – not even a hint! In this regard, the fathers agree with the New Testament writers who say nothing of such a change. Together, the witness of Scripture and of the early church is that the Sabbath was abolished and another day, with different meaning and purposes, was adopted. Indeed, there is every reason to believe that Christians worked on the Lord's Day.

Consider the following:

1. Ignatius said that the New Testament writers, "ceased to keep the Sabbath and lived by the Lord's Day, on which our life as well as theirs shone forth." Note, he said Sabbath-keeping *ceased* and, instead, the apostles and prophets kept the Lord's Day. He represented these days as entirely distinct. He said, clearly, that the Sabbath was no longer observed. He affirms not that it was moved, but that a different day was "substituted" for it.[1]

2. Justin Martyr, in his *Dialog with Trypho*, answered an objection from Trypho, a Jew, in which he complained that Christians "do not observe sabbaths." He argued that you [Christians] "do not alter your mode of living from the nations [Gentiles] in that you observe no festivals or sabbaths."[2] Justin did not contradict the charge, but explained, "But we do not trust through Moses or through the law; for then we would do the same as yourselves..." He went on to say, "For the law promulgated at Horeb is now old, and belongs to yourselves alone." Finally, he said, "The new law requires you to keep perpetual sabbath, and you, because you are idle one day,

---

base keeping the Lord's Day on the fourth commandment.

1. The Early Christian Fathers, in *the Library of Christian Classics*. Vol. 1. Westminster Press: Philadelphia (1953), p. 97.
2. Justin, "Dialog with Trypho," in *The Ante-Nicene Fathers*. Vol. 1. Eerdmans: Grand Rapids (1987), p. 199.

suppose you are pious, not discerning why this has been commanded you."[1]

From these two brief excerpts you can see how the early fathers thought. Again, like the New Testament writers, they met and worshipped on the first day. They recognized *no* other day called the Sabbath. They thought the weekly Sabbath was abrogated and that we must enter into the eternal Sabbath. And unbelievers noted the fact.

Why the Fathers?

Now, before someone objects, "We don't follow the fathers, we go only by the Scriptures," let me agree. I don't think that the fathers have any authority over us. But it is important to notice that what they said and did in no way contradicts the New Testament. In neither the Bible nor the writings of the fathers is there any indication of a change of the Sabbath to another day. And, to boot, their help is of some importance in deciding what the "Lord's Day" in Revelation means. Apart from their witness, there is no contemporary explanation – biblical or otherwise – for its meaning. Uniformly, they refer to this day as their day of worship.

Of interest to our study is the fact that immediately after the time of the apostles, until the 300s, there were some who met on both Saturday and Sunday. Obviously, those who kept both days did not think that the Sabbath and the Lord's Day were the same. The presence of the ancient practice in the church must have acted as a constant witness against the tendency to "sabbatize" the Lord's Day. When this tendency to keep the old Sabbath day continued long enough to cause alarm, the council of Laodicea (315/319 AD) outlawed the practice. Canon 29 of that council reads, "Christians must not Judaize by resting on the Sabbath, but must work that day, rather honoring the Lord's Day; and *if they can*, resting then as Christians."[2] And, the matter seemed of such importance

---

1. *Ibid.*, pp. 199, 200.
2. Alfred Barry, "The Lord's Day," in *A Dictionary of Christian Antiqui-*

that they anathematized those who continued to observe the Sabbath! It is apparent that keeping both days persisted to a time as late as the early 300s. As a result, the Greek church considered it necessary to officially oppose Sabbath-keeping.

So, by common agreement, we too believe that the Scriptures indicate that (probably under direction from the risen Christ or from the apostles, though nowhere stated) the church met on the first day of the week to commemorate the resurrection and, appropriately, called Sunday the "Lord's Day."

---

ties, Vol. II. Wm. Smith and Samuel Cheetham, eds., (Hartford: J. B. Burr Pub. Co., 1880), p. 1045.

CHAPTER THIRTEEN

Can the Sabbath be Kept Today?

When the Lord Jesus came, He brought about a whole new era. He said,

> All authority in heaven and earth has been given to Me. Go, therefore, and disciple all nations, baptizing them into the Name of the Father and of the Son and of the Holy Spirit, teaching them to observe all that I have commanded you; and remember, I will be with you always, to the close of the age.   Matthew 28:19–20

Those were His marching orders for the church. And they are words to which we must listen carefully. Let's think for a moment about some of their implications.

First, notice that Jesus mentions all nations. He was about to call a people that had not previously been His people (Romans 9:25). This was to be a new people of God composed of both Jews and Gentiles (see Ephesians 2:15, 16). Unlike Israel, it would be a spiritual kingdom, not an earthly, political one. As Jesus Himself put it: "My kingdom is not from this world...My kingdom is not from here" (John 18:36). And, as Moses did at the inauguration of the Old Covenant, when He laid the foundation of a covenant, Jesus also spoke of giving commandments to be observed ("all that I have commanded you"). Those words must not be passed over lightly. He expected His new people to be subject to His commandments as the Jews were to Moses'. Jesus' commandments replaced the Ten Commandments as they were formulated in the Mosaic code: "He is our peace, Who...has torn down the wall of enmity...by abolishing in His flesh the law of commandments with its regulations" (Ephesians 2:14, 15).

Jesus' New Commandments

As we have seen, He abolished the Old Testament law by fulfilling it. Now, His commandments consisted of new commandments that were consistent with a spiritual, worldwide kingdom. They were commandments that reached straight into the heart rather than severely regulating outward behavior, as the commandments of a political nation were bound to do (Hebrews 8:7–13).[1]

The fundamental "new commandment" that He gave to His disciples to "teach" is the commandment to "love one another" (John 13:34). Nowhere did He tell them to teach the Ten Commandments to their converts. And, yet, at the same time, this "new" commandment was not actually a new commandment, but rather, that which was "from the beginning" (II John 5). John explains: "This is love – that we walk according to His commandments" (v. 6). If the sum and substance of the law of the Ten Commandments was to love God and neighbor, how is this a "new" commandment? It is new in its formulation, and in that no one ever kept it to the full before Jesus. For the first time, we see in His life all that the commandment entails (cf. Matthew 3:15; 5:17–19). In Him, we *see* and *hear* love in action! These commandments of Christ, that could be expressed in the one word "love," were written on the tables of the heart rather than on tables of stone (II Corinthians 3:3; Jeremiah 31:31ff.).

Jesus' kingdom is a kingdom that transcends all earthly kingdoms. As the supreme Ruler of the new nation, King Jesus called out some "from every tribe and tongue and people and nation, and have made them a kingdom of priests to serve our God" (Revelation 5:9). He governs as King of Kings, Who, by His Spirit, impresses His laws upon the heart and conscience, rather than enforcing them by temporal, political power.

One Sort Doesn't Fit All

Such a spiritual kingdom, of such a people, could not be governed by a code of laws adapted to a national, temporal people such as theocratic Israel. The laws of each kingdom,

---

1. Although, of course, each of these had a spiritual meaning behind the external behavior.

and their administration, differ because the kingdoms themselves are of entirely different orders. This makes sense all around. The theocratic kingdom, which was confined to a small locality with a climate in which palm and olive trees grow, could keep a Sabbath in which it would be no hardship to go without a fire one day a week (cf. Exodus 35:3). That, today, is not possible in Alaska, Scandinavia or Afghanistan – or even here in South Carolina. Our more complex society is one in which others work on Sunday to provide electricity by which we heat our homes, light our lamps, cook on our ranges and enjoy many other conveniences.

It is obvious that, when the apostle Paul and the Christians at Troas met on the first day of the week, they did not think it necessary to forego the conveniences of their day. In Acts 20:8, we read that they lit "quite a few" lamps in the upper room where they were assembled, to listen to Paul preach. Like us, they considered illumination important to worship. Illumination, today, means electric lights – a convenience all believers, regardless of their Sabbath views, enjoy along with electric heating and cooling. And they no longer use pump organs operated by foot power (which always should have posed a problem) but electric-powered keyboards to accompany the singing of those who read hymnals by electric lighting.

Now, I could go on and on to describe many of the problem practices of those who want to keep the Old Testament Sabbath on Sundays. But, if you have thought about the problem at all, you could reiterate as many as I – or more. The main point is that in a worldwide society, like the Christian Church, a Jewish-like Sabbath simply cannot be observed. The Jews themselves, dispersed throughout the world since 70 AD, have the same problem. That is because the Old Covenant commands were designed to regulate theocratic life "in the land" of Canaan – and nowhere else (Deuteronomy 4:14). Today, we do not have a theocratic society to enforce rules and regulations such as those connected with Sabbath observance.

Of course, Jesus knew all of this and so ordered the New Covenant in a way that fits it. It was, therefore, a spiritual kingdom – composed of Jews and Gentiles – that He designed for our age. That which divided Jews from Gentiles – the law of commandments with its regulations – was done away with. We must not attempt to re-establish it in any form, lest we divide that which Jesus has united (Ephesians 2:14, 15).

CHAPTER FOURTEEN

What of the Lord's Day?

In keeping with the historical precedent of observing the Lord's Day, it is important that we should not observe it as a Sabbath. Paul Jewett's comment is succinct, but telling: "The Lord's Day was not called the Sabbath for over a thousand years."[1] He is right.

How to Observe it

"Well, if Christians are not to observe the Lord's Day as a Sabbath, how should we observe it?" From the New Testament data, it seems that the first day of the week was the church's day for worship. On it, Christians assembled, they sang, they prayed, they listened to the exposition and application of the Scriptures, they received the sacraments, and they laid aside money for the needy.

Is the church obligated to do these things on that day? May not one worship with his family or a small group in his own home? The problem of Christians who do not regularly meet together arose early on and was addressed in the Bible: "We must not abandon the practice of meeting together, as some are in the habit of doing" (Hebrews 10:25). Why did he think that this was important? The writer continues, "We must encourage each other, and all the more as you see the day drawing near." How important was this matter? Was a Christian obliged to meet only on Sunday? Was it wrong to be flexible about this?

Meeting Together

Well, first, let me say that the above quotation from Hebrews is pretty clear. It speaks of some who developed the bad habit of neglecting – or even abandoning – the regular meetings of the church. The writer sees this as a time when

---

1. Paul K. Jewett. *The Lord's Day*. Wm. B. Eerdmans: Grand Rapids (1971), p. 151.

various forms of needed encouragement should take place. The word translated "encourage" is *parakaleo*. It is a comprehensive term that means "to provide whatever sort of assistance is necessary." The writer of Hebrews was aware of the impending destruction of Jerusalem, and it was in this context that he offered encouragement. When he mentioned the "day drawing near," it was to that destruction he was referring. Jesus predicted the destruction of Jerusalem in Matthew 24 (cf. Luke 21), when it was clear that the last days of the Old Testament era were running out. But it is not only because of the "impending crisis" (as Paul called it in I Corinthians 7:26) that the writer of Hebrews offers this encouragement. No, meeting together had always been necessary; but it was *especially* so in such hard times.

This encouragement that the author of Hebrews was promoting is, in part, mentioned in the previous verse: "and let us give thought to ways of stimulating one another to love and fine deeds" (Hebrews 10:24). The word "stimulating" is especially strong. It can even mean "to irritate" or "to provoke." The idea is that we need prodding if we are to become more loving and perform fine deeds. If that is going to happen, it will take thought and planning. That is why we are told to "give thought" about ways of doing these things. Presumably, to obey this injunction, we must give time to thought and planning. And much of this encouragement would take place during the weekly service. What a tragedy it is when people who come to church regularly hear from the pulpit nothing more than academic pap that fails to truly encourage and stimulate them to live for Christ! How sad when people come and leave without spending time with other believers fellowshipping in ways that also stimulate fine deeds. Regular services, then, are not merely an option. They are essential!

When to Meet

So, Christians must frequent church services. But must they meet on the first day of the week? There is no absolute command to do so. We do it, as we saw, out of example rather than precept. And, if there is no pressing need to do otherwise, it surely is the time for Christians to meet. It is conceivable, however, in some irregular circumstances that services might be held on another day that the elders deem the only possible time to do so. If, out of necessity, in some unusual situation, Christians do meet on another day, it isn't sin to do so. That is because sin is disobedience to God. But we have neither a command to meet on the first day nor a prohibition from meeting on some other day.

So on the Lord's Day, we assemble together to participate in all of the joint activities of the Church of Jesus Christ. There are to be no "lone wolf" Christians.[1] We cannot make it alone. How do we know that? Because God designed us that way. We were created social beings, and as believers we need to fellowship with those who are a part of the society of faith.

Insofar as they referred to the Lord's Day, the early church fathers unanimously declared that it was celebrated on the day Jesus rose from the dead. It has been called "the Christian's weekly Easter." Just as the Sabbath commemorated the creation, the Lord's Day commemorated the new creation brought about by the risen Lord.

A Holy Day?

Yes and no. Insofar as there are no days more holy than others in this era, the answer is no. In that every day ought to be holy, the answer is yes. Paul envisions treating every day *alike* to God's honor (Romans 14:5). Indeed, that is the position of the stronger brother in the passage. And, it is how we should view life today. There is no longer a holy temple. Our church buildings are just that – buildings in which we meet. They are not temples set aside as more holy than other buildings. We have no holy things like the pots and pans that were used in the temple. There is no particular holy place like the

---

1. Calvin thought the church should meet more than once a week. There is no biblical warrant for refusing to do so. Indeed, the early church met at other times as well (Acts 2:46; 5:42).

holy of holies (cf. John 4:21–24). All of that is done away with in Christ. Our bodies, which are the temple of the Spirit in this era, are to be kept holy. But there are no holy places, no holy things, no holy ceremonies. The era prophesied by Zechariah has now come, when every pot and pan in town is holy, and even the bells on the horses are holy! (Zechariah 14:20, 21).

What does the Lord's Day Mean?

The phrase "the Lord's day" occurs in Revelation 1:10 ("I was in the Spirit on the Lord's day"). It refers to the Lord Jesus' day. Jesus is the "Yahweh" of the Old Testament, Who is the "Lord" of the New. Passages referring to "Yahweh" in the Old Testament are attributed to Him in the New. The title given to the first day of the week possibly refers to the day of Jesus' resurrection, but if it takes the parallel form of I Corinthians 11:20 ("the Lord's Supper") it might indicate that Jesus gave the church this day as He gave them His supper. Be that as it may, in later usage it always refers to the resurrection.

Perhaps the finest summary of these facts is found in Calvin's sermon on Galatians 4:8–10, where, among other things, he says,

> We today need to pay most careful attention to the fact that if we fall away in the slightest degree from the truth of the gospel, we are departing from Jesus Christ Himself. Yes, it is true that we have set days upon which we meet together, but not in the same manner as the Jews. What is the difference? We do not observe them as ceremonies. Under the law, if a person so much as lifted a hammer to a piece of wood on the day of rest, or did his household duties it was a crime punishable by death. If a person dared boil a pot of water, God commanded that he should be put to death. Now, these harsh laws[1] did not exist

---

1. Paul calls them "weak and pitiful elements," and says that one who

because God delighted in idleness! No, rather, they had spiritual significance; it was as if God was saying, "I have given you Sabbath days to observe that you might know that I am the God who sanctifies you." We enjoy the same sanctification today, but not through observing figures as our forefathers did, for this is to ignore the role of the Lord Jesus Christ.[1]

---

adopts them returns to bondage (Galatians 4:9–11). The Jewish ordinances were weak and pitiful in that they were rudimentary rituals (*stoicheia*) that had no power to save or sanctify. To adopt them was to go backwards into slavery similar to that from which Christ freed us.

1. John Calvin, *Sermons on Galatians.* Edinburgh: The Banner of Truth Trust (1977), p. 397.

CHAPTER FIFTEEN

That Passage in James

There is a passage that at first glance might seem to substantiate the idea that the Ten Commandments have been continued into New Testament times without significant alteration. This passage is James 2:8–13. Which reads as follows:

> If, however, you really fulfill the royal law, which according to the Scriptures is, "You must love your neighbor as yourself," you do well; but if you show favoritism, you commit sin and are convicted by the law as transgressors. So, whoever keeps the whole law, but stumbles in one point, has become guilty of all. The same One Who said, "Don't commit adultery," also said, "Don't murder." So if you don't commit adultery but murder, you have become a transgressor of the law. Speak and act as those who are about to be judged by the law of freedom.[1] I say this because judgment will be without mercy to him who doesn't show mercy. Mercy triumphs over judgment.

Now, let's look at the context of the passage. James was speaking of showing favoritism to a church visitor because he is well-dressed (and obviously well-heeled!) while, at the same time, paying scant attention to a poor man. He would allow no excuse for doing this; he declared it a sin. If anyone should protest that he did nothing wrong since, after all, he *was* treating one man well, James says that is no excuse for treating another poorly. A good deed doesn't cancel out a bad one. To *illustrate* this principle, he mentions the Old Testament Law (his readers were converted Jews who would understand). If a person were to keep all the other commandments (he

---

1. In contrast to the "burdensome" Mosaic law.

offers this merely as a hypothetical example[1]) but were to stumble in only one, he would still be guilty of having broken the Law.

I once stored a large mirror in the garage, but one small corner of it was broken. It was only a corner – but the *mirror* was broken. It was useless. That is how it is with sin. One sin ruins everything. Going through nine green lights doesn't make up for going through one red light! It's that one red light, that one broken corner of the mirror, that matter.

To *really* fulfill the royal (kingly) Law, which is to love one's neighbor as one's self (evidently as his readers claimed to), is to do well, James says. But to show favoritism is sin. Why? Because the very law that was fulfilled in one instance convicts you of sin in the other. One could do all sorts of good things for the rich man, but to neglect the poor person at the same time is to fail to love him. In effect, James asks, "Since when does doing good things for one person excuse you from doing good for another?"

The Ten Commandments Used Illustratively

James turned to the Ten Commandments only as an illustration (v. 11). God gave both the command about adultery and the one about murder. If you keep one but not the other, you have broken the Law. You are guilty of all because the whole is no longer intact, any more than the mirror or your driving record. You are not allowed to pick and choose those situations in which you will obey and those in which you will not.

He continues, "speak and act like those who are about to be judged by the law of freedom (or liberty)." God will judge them, James wants them to know, but not by the Ten Commandments, from which he has just given them an example. Calvin says that "He means by the word *liberty* that we are freed from the rigor of the [Old Testament] law."[2] We must freely obey God but not merely because of the judgment that

---

1. He recognizes that we all stumble (sin) in many ways (James 3:2).
2. John Calvin, *Commentary on James*, p. 307. Cf. Galatians 5:1, 18.

falls upon those who break His law. We should love someone because he is our neighbor. If we were to be judged by the Law, there would be no mercy (v. 13). God's mercy – in Christ – triumphs over judgment. By Him we were set free from judgment. But, because this is the case, we must keep Paul's admonition in mind: "You were called to freedom, brothers; only don't allow the flesh to take advantage of this freedom. Instead, through love we must serve one another" (Galatians 5:13). So, in dealing with others, we must treat them as God treats us – with mercy.

Obviously, then, the passage understood rightly had nothing to do with the survival of the Ten Commandments. We must not appeal to this passage in the debate. There is one other passage, however, to be considered in this discussion. We shall do so in the next chapter.

CHAPTER SIXTEEN

Matthew 5:17–20

Let's begin by reading the passage:

> Don't think that I came to abolish the Law or the Prophets; I didn't come to abolish but to fulfill. What I say to you is certain – until heaven and earth pass away,[1] not the smallest letter or the smallest part of a letter will in any way pass away from the law until everything has taken place.

Now, this Scripture surely must be considered. Doesn't it say that nothing in the Mosaic Law will be abolished ("destroyed" or "thrown down" – ever)? Well, no; it doesn't. "No?" you ask. "It seems plain as the nose on my face that it does – and I have quite a snoz!" Well, I won't argue about the shape of your nose, but I do want to talk to you about how you are shaping (actually *mis*shaping) the passage.

The phrase "The Law and the Prophets" was well recognized as a title for the Old Testament books as a whole – not for the Ten Commandments. And when the word "Law" occurs in a passage growing out of a former contextual phrase that was used to designate the whole Old Testament (as it does here), it must be understood as referring to the same thing in a shorter form. So, what Jesus was saying was that no one – including Me – can tear down the Scriptures any more than he can cause heaven and earth to pass away. Indeed, the Scriptures will stand until every type and shadow has been completely fulfilled.

Jesus did not want to be known as a revolutionary who had come to destroy what God has set up. Instead of showing disrespect for the Bible, He affirmed its truth and declared "the Scripture cannot be relaxed" (John 10:35). Rather than destroying the Scriptures, He was fulfilling them. The two

---

1. A proverbial expression meaning "never."

things are quite distinct and should not be confused. Fulfilling is the ultimate way of respecting and establishing the Bible.

What "Fulfill" Means

The use of the word "fulfill" here is something like its use in our expression "that fulfilled all of my expectations." That is to say, if we are talking of a meal as doing so, we mean nothing could have been changed for the better. Everything – without omission – was provided and was of superb quality. It was *entirely* up to snuff. So, in quality and quantity, the meal fulfilled all expectations. To change the figure, the Old Testament is also like a container that was finally being filled to the brim by what Christ did and taught. When He was finished, not a drop more could be added.

The word translated "commandment" is *entole*, which means "ordinance, injunction." Jesus said that He would set aside nothing that God ordered or required, as the Pharisees did. They "relaxed" (*luo*) the commandments, shaping them to suit themselves. The phrase "until everything takes place" means "until all is accomplished." Everything that God ordained will come to pass without fail. But note, the fulfillment of the Old Testament Scriptures had already begun to take place when He spoke these words. Christ now makes it clear that His teaching agrees perfectly with the Law and the Prophets and, along with His perfect life, brings complete fulfillment of the predictions found in them. Teaching the inner, intended meaning of the Old Testament does not destroy it or tear it down. When He lives and reveals the truths behind the signs, types and symbols, He is fulfilling them. He brings them into clearer focus by showing their full, intended meanings and purposes. He does this by relegating the ceremonies to the shadows – which is now their proper place. They had to fade away once the Sun of Righteousness arose in midday splendor.

John's Place in This

In Luke 16:16, 17, Jesus connects the fulfillment of the Law with the time of John the Baptist (see also Matthew

11:12, 13). Here we read that the Law and the Prophets were preached until John came; from his time on God's kingdom has been preached. That change is important to note. The passage continues, "But it is easier for heaven and earth to pass away than for one dot of the law to fall from it."

That the Old Testament was preached *until* John (the last of the Old Testament prophets who stood on the razor's edge between the two eras) indicates that there was a change in preaching after him. Now, it was the coming kingdom that both he and Jesus preached (John announcing first that it was "at hand," Jesus, later saying it had arrived). Does that mean that the Old Testament no longer has value for us and should not be preached? Of course not! What it means is that though the new message takes away nothing from the older one, it adds much. That is why the old should no longer be preached as it once had been. There is now new light shining that brings out the fuller spiritual, eternal meaning that was always there, but often hidden by the shadows. As Jesus put it in Luke 5:36–39, there is new wine that must be poured into new wineskins. The old ones cannot contain the fermenting wine that would burst them. Old ceremonies and ways of preaching the good news had to give way to the new greater reality.

So, Jesus' saying about fulfilling the Law and the Commandments had to do with the Ten Commandments only tangentially. He was speaking of the Bible of His time as a whole. In linking His saying with the change in preaching that occurred with John's coming, He showed that a radical re-orientation, consistent with fulfilling everything in the old era, was taking place. That fits, exactly, with all that we have seen of Sabbath-keeping. Jesus is the Rest that the world longed for.

CHAPTER SEVENTEEN

Living Like a Gentile

One of the most fascinating passages in the New Testament and one that is of importance to our study is Galatians 2:14. Paul confronted Peter because he engaged in politically correct behavior. Before some Judaizers appeared on the scene, Peter ate with Gentiles, "but when they came, he withdrew and separated himself" out of fear of the "circumcision party" Galatians 2:12. Others were adversely affected by his deplorable example. So Paul took him on: "I said, in front of everybody, 'If you, who are a Jew live like a Gentile and don't live like a Jew, how can you compel Gentiles to live like Jews?'"

Obviously, this passage explains much about how difficult it was to get some of the Jews to give up their Jewish ways. Even though Peter had experienced a divine revelation that it was proper for him to eat with Gentiles (Acts 10), under pressure he fell back into his old patterns and had to be rebuked by Paul. The difficulty encountered is similar to the problem today of getting Gentiles to live like Gentiles with reference to the Sabbath. At best, it may be said that many in our time are like the "Proselytes of the Gate" (or Gentile "God-fearers" as they were also called) who, while not submitting to circumcision, believed in Yahweh and kept the Sabbath. You might call them "Jewtiles." Like them, many Christians today have adopted a blend of New and Old Testament requirements for their lives.

Judaizing

Much in the book of Galatians is of concern to us. The problem discussed was Judaizing. There were some who taught that Gentiles had to become Jews before they could become Christians. This meant that they had to adopt Jewish ways. The three Jewish distinctives that stand out in the letter are circumcision, refusing to eat with Gentiles, and the keeping of days (Galatians 4:10).

In summarizing the rebuke that Paul gave to Peter, he says

that he asked him, "If you, who are a Jew, live like a Gentile, and don't live like a Jew, how can you compel Gentiles to live like Jews?" The fact that before the Judaizers appeared Peter lived *like a Gentile and not like a Jew* is very significant. To engage in the customs of the Jews was what set apart the Jews from the Gentiles in any community. One of the most conspicuous marks that separated them was the Sabbath. Indeed, the Sabbath was the sign whereby God "sanctified" (i.e., "set apart") Israel from other people (Exodus 31:13; Ezekiel 20:12, 20). From every point of view it would seem that, when living like a Gentile, Peter could not have been keeping the Sabbath.

Shedding Jewish Ways

But, that isn't all that Paul had in mind when he said that Peter had been living like a Gentile; he meant that there was no discernible difference in his lifestyle (apart from sin, of course) from that of the Gentiles around him at Antioch. It meant that he had shed the Jewish practices mentioned in Galatians. If, however, the Christians had merely merged the Sabbath and the first day, they might not be living *exactly* like Jews – but they certainly would not have been living like Gentiles.

How do we know that living like a Jew included Sabbath-keeping? Because Paul made a point of it (cf. Galatians 4:8–11). His words, written against Judaizing tendencies, make it quite clear that he was deeply concerned about the keeping of days. He calls this going back to the "weak and pitiful elements" and declares, "I am afraid that I have labored among you in vain." His labor, therefore, included abolishing holy days. Obviously, if he had shed the customs of his past and was, like Peter, living like the Gentiles who kept no Jewish days, there was reason for his concern. To observe days was to fail to live according to one's freedom in Christ (cf. vv. 8, 9).

Paul Did the Same

In I Corinthians 9:20, Paul explains that in evangelizing he "became like a Jew...I became like one who is under the law," and in verse 21 he said that to those "without the law" he "became like one who is without law..." That is, like Peter, "as a Gentile." Now, think about what this means:

1. If Paul also lived as a Gentile (i.e., "without the law") would he "break" the Sabbath by doing so?[1]

2. If Paul *"became* like a Jew" (v. 20) in order to evangelize Jews, living like a Jew must not have been his normal life-style. Otherwise, he would not have had to "become" like a Jew.

3. When Paul declared that he was "not without God's law," but was "within the law (*ennomos*) of Christ" (v. 21), he was explaining that he kept God's law by obeying Christ's law – presumably, the law of love.[2]

Gentile Living Today

Of great concern to us today ought to be whether or not we are living like Jews or like Gentiles. After abolishing in His [Christ's] flesh the law of commandments with its regulations" God made of Jews and Gentiles "one new man" (Ephesians 2:15). This "new man" in Christ, today's church member, would have to look either like a Jew, a Gentile, or a blend of both. But we see by Peter's example before compromising, that contrary to the Sabbatarian view (which is a blend), the proper way for the "new man" to live is like a Gentile. Those who keep the weekly Sabbath, teaching that the day of the week is virtually all that has changed, could hardly say that. In this regard, they are actually living like

---

1. A serious question to ponder: Would a Sabbatarian do the same today? Dr. William Evans, professor of Bible at Erskine College and currently moderator of the Associate Reformed Synod, writes, "The old distinctions of the Mosaic law between Jews and Gentiles had been decisively transcended by the work of Christ. And so, when Paul evangelized Gentiles he lived as a Gentile and when he evangelized Jews he lived as a Jew (I Corinthians 9:19–23)." Cf. *ARP Magazine,* July 2005, p. 5.

2. For an outstanding exegesis of this passage, see Charles Hodge, *An Exposition of 1 and 2 Corinthians.* Wilmington: Sovereign Grace Publishers (1972), p. 97.

Jews. Their deep concern is to retain – rather than abolish – most of the Jewish elements of Sabbath observance so that, by keeping it intact, they may be able to live like Jews. Now, they wouldn't express it that way, of course. But that is precisely what they are doing. Evidence of this is their consistent application of Old Testament passages that explain Jewish life on the Sabbath to Christians. The fundamental question is, then, "When it comes to Sabbath-keeping, are you living like a Jew or a Gentile?"

CHAPTER EIGHTEEN

Was the Sabbath Set Aside for Corporate Worship?

Was the Sabbath set aside for corporate worship? Again, where is the evidence? Those who believe that the substance of the Sabbath was carried over to the Lord's Day frequently suggest that the church worships corporately on Sunday because the Jews did on Saturday. If there were evidence to show that God required corporate worship as part of the Sabbath, it would still not prove that the supposed change of day necessarily brought with it elements of worship. At best, it would prove that similarities exist in that respect. And, for that matter, even if corporate worship is *not* a carry-over from the Jewish Sabbath, it is certainly proper to worship on the first day of the week. That is not what is under contention. But where is the evidence of a command for corporate Sabbath worship? Again, we are faced with assertions, not biblical proof.

Rest is Commanded

The fourth commandment, in both Exodus and Deuteronomy commands rest, not worship. There is no command for worship, let alone corporate worship. The fact that many years after the Mosaic Covenant was given, in New Testament times the Jews are found meeting in synagogs (literally, "places where people come together") proves nothing of the sort. It seems that during the exile, without the benefit of their temple, the Jews developed synagog worship, which they brought back to the land after the exile. But there is no solid biblical support for this explanation of the synagog's origin.

The Manna Incident

The one command that may be even remotely relevant to our discussion – in a negative way – is found in the "preview sabbath" that took place during the gathering of Manna. It reads, "Everyone is to stay where he is on the seventh day; no one is to go out" (Exodus 16:29). It appears that, rather than gather for worship on this proto-sabbath, one must stay home. Of course, contemplation and family worship might take place, which would be admirable – but not commanded, or even so much as hinted at.

How the Sabbath was Holy

When the Sabbath is called a "holy" day (Exodus 31:14; 35:2) it means the Sabbath was to be observed *differently* from the six other days that preceded it. It was set apart from regular work. The word has nothing to do with corporate worship. The day was "hallowed" (made different, special). The term "holy" was applied to anything "set apart" – even to utensils in the temple. The seventh day was to be treated differently from other days because it belonged peculiarly to the Lord. The Sabbath was to the week what the holy of holies was to the rest of the temple. Every day was God's day, but the seventh day was especially so. What made it holy was the fact that it was a day of rest from weekday labors.

It is not unimportant that rest rather than worship was emphasized everywhere in relation to the seventh day. The penalties for breaking the Sabbath had nothing to do with failure to worship, but with failure to rest. One cannot fault New Testament Jews for putting the emphasis on rest, and seeking not to transgress God's commandment by working. Their problem was that they missed the true intent of the Sabbath rest, while legalistically adding to the Scripture's rules that they casuistically framed to enforce it. Legalism always adds to what God commands, as if His instructions were inadequate. In time, these additions, rather than becoming mere suggestions to help one obey, became at least as important as the command itself.

Holy Convocations

In Leviticus 23:3 we read,

> For six days work may be done, but on the seventh day there must be a Sabbath of complete

rest, a sacred assembly. You are not to do any work; it is a Sabbath to the Lord wherever you live.   (HCSB)

Was this "convocation" a religious assembly of people in a community? It could have been. But the fact is that we know very little about the convocations mentioned. The word convocation ("gathering") often refers to a universal gathering of God's people in Jerusalem. But such a weekly temple gathering would have been impossible. Every Jew (or, least every male) had to come to Jerusalem three times a year for special festivals. But every week? No. Such weekly travel would be impossible.

Could it refer to a gathering of people in a given area? That certainly is more likely. We know that at a later time the Jews met in "places of prayer" (seemingly where no synagog existed). These were informal – not prescribed – Sabbath gatherings.[1] We know that the Sabbath was to be a time of fellowship, feasting rather than fasting[2] (see Luke 14:1) and joy (Isaiah 58:13). Most likely, the Sabbath convocation was just such a time. The period of rest provided a special ("holy") opportunity to gather for fellowship and informal worship.

Although there was no requirement for corporate worship attached to the convocation, it is possible that there was some teaching and prayer at such local gatherings. It may be that these developed into synagog meetings that evolved during the exile. II Kings 4:22–25 may provide a hint of teaching at localized Sabbath gatherings. In this passage, the Shunamite's husband asks his wife why she wanted to go see Elisha, "the man of God, since it was "neither new moon or Sabbath" (v. 23). This seems to indicate that there was a practice of the sort on such occasions.

The significant fact, however, is that *prescribed* worship

---

1. Acts 16:13. N.B., it was on a Sabbath that the Jews gathered at the river.
2. Jesus had no hesitancy about attending a dinner on the Sabbath (see also Isaiah 58:13).

took place at the temple, not in the local community.[1] Specified corporate worship, in addition to the daily and weekly sacrifices, was conducted at annual affairs, at the three yearly feasts. So, it seems apparent that, beyond the temple sacrifices, no obligatory corporate worship was required during the weekly Sabbath. There is no biblical support, therefore, for the often-made claim that Christian Sunday worship was a carry-over from the seventh day Sabbath. There was nothing to carry over!

The biblical evidence leads us to conclude that Hendrik Bosman's words are correct: "the ordinary Israelites knew of no specific religious practices peculiar to the Sabbath, and that rest was the only, or at least, the prominent Sabbath prescription they adhered to."[2]

---

1. In Ezekiel 46:3, 4, 9 we are looking at special, not weekly, Sabbaths.
2. In Willem Van Gemeren, ed., *The New International Dictionary of Old Testament Theology and Exegesis.* Zondervan: Grand Rapids (1977). p. 1160. This Dictionary is the latest and most scholarly truly biblical work of its kind that is currently available.

CHAPTER NINETEEN

What About Antinomianism?

"What on earth is Antinomianism? And what has it to do with our discussion?" Really, nothing, as I hope you will see. But some may think that it does. So here goes...

The Term

I said that Christ fulfilled all of the Mosaic law which, as a result, became obsolete (actually, the writer to the Hebrews was the one who said it: Hebrews 8:13). And I said that we are not under the old Mosaic Covenant (actually, Paul said that). Therefore, I concluded that we are not obligated to keep the Ten Commandments as they were written on the stone tablets constituting the essence of the Jewish national covenant. Rather, a New Covenant has replaced the Old, and today we are obligated to keep the terms of the New Covenant in Christ (actually the writer of Hebrews said that too!).

Now, to say that the Commandments – as they were formulated when codified – have no authority for us, but were removed along with the Ark in which they were placed, makes some shudder. Immediately, they mentally picture people running amuck because they have no rule by which to live. They quickly find one word forming on their lips – Antinomianism!

What is it? Literally it means "against, or instead of law." The antinomian is one who advocated vagaries like that set forth in the faulty slogan, "No creed but Christ; no law but love." According to A.A. Hodge, antinomianism is "a horrible doctrine" and an "abominable heresy" which teaches that "because Christ has fulfilled all of the moral law in behalf of all of the elect...they are released from all obligations to fulfill its precepts as a standard of character and action."[1] Surely, no one I know wants to be guilty of such things. Least of all, the writer! Hodge further explicates: they [antinomians] all

---

1. *Outlines of Theology.* Eerdmans: Grand Rapids (1957), p. 404.

agree in teaching that Christians in this life are no longer under obligation to fulfill the Adamic law of absolute moral perfection."[1] I am well aware of the fact that I have opened myself up to the charge of Antinomianism. So, let me show you why it is wrong to think of what I have written as such.

No Antinomianism Here

Take Hodge's second comment first. Do I believe that not only Adam, but all of his posterity, are obligated to fulfill God's perfect law? Of course I do (even though there are "Reformed" people today who don't. Don't place me in their camp!) If it were not so, why else did Jesus die? He died to save sinful persons like me who have not fulfilled those obligations. The covenant of works, under which Adam was placed, is still active. And if it were not for God's grace, I would be damned by it. God had to send His Son in my stead to do by His active obedience what I, as a sinner, could not do. His righteousness, by grace through faith, has been attributed to me. He alone is my hope in life and death! But His grace, rather than relieving me from responsibility to please Him, all the more obligates me to do so.

Now, consider Hodge's first comment. He says that antinomians claim that because of what Jesus did for the elect, they are under no obligation to fulfill the Law's precepts regarding character and actions. Of course, they are so obligated as I just said. Every believer ought to live like Jesus Christ. But that doesn't mean that he must obey the Ten Word Code *as formulated*. The Mosaic law, in that form, was unknown to Adam and the Patriarchs. Were they antinomians? Certainly not. In spite of the lack of the Ten Commandment code, Enoch "walked with God" (Genesis 5:22). His character and actions must have conformed to God's will to a large extent as, indeed, ours should today. The commonly used biblical word "walk" in the passage (as elsewhere) has to do with a manner of life that pleases God.

---

1. *Ibid.*, p. 526.

Antinomians do not like commandments. But those of us who seek to serve Jesus follow His Law (Galatians 6:2). The two great commandments are a summary of His will. Misunderstanding of love – the predominant word in these commandments – has led some to deny the need to follow Christ's *commandments* (as such). That is, of course, self-contradictory. True biblical love is not amorphous (John 14:15). Referring to "apostolic precepts," Horatius Bonar wrote,

> These are the *commandments* of the Holy Ghost, and they are LAW just as truly as that which was proclaimed in Horeb amid fire and darkness. And the true question with us (as we have seen) is not whether we are to obey this law or that law, but *any law at all* (emphasis his).[1]

When Jeremiah spoke of the law "written on the heart," he had in mind that in days to come the Christian would obey the law of Christ as it is set forth in the New Testament. Love begets desire and ability to obey (Romans 5:5); obedience begets love, and so on. In place of Israel's national law code, God's laws for life for us are bundled up in the word "love." Love is living like Christ by following His example and obeying His commandments.

Antinomians do not believe that they must obey or repent when they fail to do so. They think that they merely need to thank God that all has been taken care of in Christ. I refuted this dangerous opinion in detail in *The Theology of Christian Counseling* (pp. 196ff.). In the Antinomian view, there is no place for repentance, forgiveness and the changes that must accompany it. God requires every believer, however, "to observe all things" that Christ commanded. That is certainly no antinomian statement! Rather, it includes repentance and obedience.

The New Testament is far from being an antinomian book. When we obey Christ it is because He gives us "both the willingness and the ability *to do the things that please Him*"

---

1. *God's Way of Holiness*. The Moody Press: Chicago (n.d.), p. 92.

(Philippians 2:13). That statement of Paul is similar to Jeremiah's predictions about the law written on the heart (Jeremiah 31:33). According to Paul, we must "walk in a way that is worthy of the Lord, *pleasing Him* in everything." In doing so, we will bear "the fruit of every sort of good work" (Colossians 1:10). Obviously, pleasing Christ involves *being* and *doing* those things that *please Him*. But we must never attempt to become "doers" of the royal law either in our own wisdom or strength.[1] It is possible, increasingly, to become more like Christ because the Holy Spirit Who wrote the law on our hearts also strengthens us to obey it (Romans 5:5; Hebrews 8:8–13). Like Paul, we must "make it our ambition *to please Him*" (II Corinthians 5:9).

But how does one learn what it is that *pleases* Christ? Paul wrote, "we ask and urge you…as you learned from us how you ought to walk and *please* God…that you continue to do so even more and more" (I Thessalonians 4:1). It is obedience to Christ and the "apostolic precepts," as Bonar called Scripture, that pleases Him. So, it is clear to all who have the eyes to see – and who keep them wide open as they read – that the position taken in this book may by no means be fairly called Antinomianism. If any claim that it is, please set them straight. One final word: the danger in misunderstanding and applying the Scriptures today, I might suggest, is not so much Antinomianism as Legalism.

---

1. According to Hebrews 13:21, God "equips" us with "every good thing for doing His will, producing in us what pleases Him." We do His will, but He gives us what is necessary to do it. Thus the human and the divine come together to produce holy living, according to Christ's will which is set forth in His commandments.

CHAPTER TWENTY

Rest Isn't Optional

We saw that God doesn't require Christians to keep the Sabbath as it was promulgated in the decalog, and that the seventh day was set apart from the other days of the week to commemorate God's creation. But Jesus also taught that the Sabbath was made for man's benefit. What made it special was that it forbade work of the usual sort. There is no command to set it apart for corporate worship. And from that fact we drew the necessary conclusion that this distinguishes the Christian Lord's Day from the Jewish Sabbath.[1]

Old Testament Idea of Rest

The concept of rest that pervades the Old Testament is "rest" in the land of Canaan (see Deuteronomy 12:10; 25:19; Joshua 1:13, 15; 11:23; 21:44; 22:4; 23:1 – all important passages). It is described as "rest on every side," from "enemies," and from "war." This is the rest to which Hebrews refers when denying that this earthly rest is that which "remains for the people of God" (Hebrews 4:8, 9). Rest, as we see, has within it the ideas of peace and quietness, with the absence of turmoil (cf. Job 3:26; Isaiah 14:7). And in addition, there is the thought of security as over against fear (Deuteronomy 33:12; Job 11:18; 24:23; Psalm 16:9). Ultimately, the final rest is found in God alone (Psalm 62:5).

The idea of receiving rest at death is frequently found (cf. Deuteronomy 31:16; Isaiah 57:2). Rest of mind (literally "heart") as well as rest of the body is included (Ecclesiastes 2:23). There is also the notion of refreshment from various trials (Exodus 23:12; Jeremiah 6:16. See especially, Matthew 11:28, 29). And the wicked are said to have "no rest" (Isaiah 57:21. See also Revelation 14:11 where this fact is given an eternal emphasis).

---

1. Those Judaizing Christians who met on both days must surely have known this.

Rest in the New Testament

Having reached our understanding of the abolishment of the Sabbath we did not conclude, however, that there is no need for rest, and no imperative to rest from toil. Our findings do not lend support to the workaholic. Rather, in the New Covenant, the moral obligation to rest rises to a higher level as Christians are commanded to care for the body as the temple of the Spirit Who dwells in each member of the church.

Rest is essential to a well-functioning body through which the Spirit may carry out his sanctifying and edifying purposes. That is a strong reason for securing rest. In a world of sin, with its effects on the body (disease, injury, sickness and the like) we can never completely avoid physical problems. Far from it. But properly resting the body is something over which we ordinarily have a measure of control. We are not like the people of God under slavery in Egypt! Cessation from work, then, allows the body to recuperate from the wear and tear of work against the thorns. Resting it is one way to "glorify God in your body" (I Corinthians 6:20).

Sleep is Necessary

If anything abuses the body so that it fails to function as intended, it is sleep deprivation. Every experienced counselor knows that many supposed "psychopathic" problems are actually the result of significant sleep loss. Studies have shown that two to four days of sleep deprivation may lead to the same effects as hallucinogenic drugs in some people. In other more or less serious cases, failure to sleep may result in injuries at work, difficulty to maintain one's composure under stress and the like. Sleep – one example of bodily rest – is essential.

Failure to Treat Sickness or Injury

The body (which includes the brain) is the means by which one's spirit (or soul) contacts the physical world. By means of the body a person receives impressions from the world, and then acts upon them. The soul of the believer, in turn, is also in contact with the Holy Spirit, Who works through the believer to bring about His will in the believer's life and the world around him. When the body is impaired, the soul is also impaired in its relationship to the physical world. One may not be able to learn, think, or act in ways that he might if he were not hampered by sickness. The Christian, therefore, must make all necessary efforts to keep his body in the best possible shape. That may include medical treatment. Physicians, as a result, are not engaged in physical ministry exclusively, as some may think. Because by means of healing they enable Christians to grow spiritually and to serve more faithfully, they are engaged in spiritual work – whether or not they know it.

Thus, rest enables the sanctifying work of the Spirit to take place. There should be no doubt about the fact that resting is one of the ways in which a believer cares for the temple of the Spirit. Having tasted something of God's eternal rest, he is not required to rest one day in seven; but he must remain clear of sin, which takes its toll on the body. Periods of rest may be interspersed in a one-day-in-seven manner, or in ways that are equally appropriate to a different schedule. Neither is specified in the New Testament. But the believer must rest; rest isn't optional.

CHAPTER TWENTY ONE

Conclusion

Paul Jewett wrote. "The Sabbath above all other enactments of the law forced itself upon the notice of one's neighbors." This means that the Sabbath was significant for its sign value, as we have seen. He went on to say, "the observance of the Sabbath was the touchstone of Israel's witness to the living God."[1] Do Christians want Sabbath-keeping to be the touchstone of their witness? Considering the zeal for Sabbath-keeping that some have, you would imagine that they would answer, "Just so!" After our study, I hope that you will say "No!"

We wouldn't be ashamed for Sabbath-keeping to be the outstanding factor visible to our neighbors, were that a proper biblical emphasis. But, instead, we find a different one. Surely, we remember God as Creator, our Redeemer, and the One who made us a different people. But none of these factors is the touchstone. What, then, is? Jesus told us, "Everybody will know that you are My disciples by this: that you have love for one another" (John 13:35). That's our touchstone – the one by which we should long for the world to know us as God's own.

Like Peter, we live as Gentiles. Old distinguishing features have faded. Instead, there is to be an inward quality that outwardly shows itself in love. Indeed, in the days of the early church this quality was recognized. Tertullian wrote that the heathen said about Christians, "Behold, how they love one another."[2] And Lucian said, "It is incredible to see the ardor with which the people of that religion help each other in their wants. They spare nothing."[3]

---

1. *Op. cit.*, p. 34. Jewett's words echo Ezekiel 20:9–26. Profaning the Sabbath was a profaning of God's Name before the nations, "among whom they lived" (v. 9). It was the sign of the "sanctified" (set apart) nation. See vv. 12, 13, 14, 20, 22.
2. In Philip Schaff, *History of the Christian Church*. Vol. II. AP&A, n.d., p. 167.
3. *Ibid.*, p. 168.

Love is Central

Now, of course, Christians are often indistinguishable from others when they fail to keep Christ's commandments. But when they are at their best – as they usually are in times of persecution – the touchstone of love is apparent. The aim of Christ's commandments is "love" (I Timothy 1:5). The Law is "good," but it must be used "lawfully" (I Timothy 1:8). Judaizers don't. Paul associates its lawful use with his "healthy teaching" (I Timothy 1:9–11).

Sabbatarianism leaves too much unexplained. Since the burden of proof is upon those who claim that we must observe the Sabbath Day, it is incumbent upon them to offer evidence. A great number of unfounded claims over the years have led people to believe that there must be a large amount of evidence for Sabbath-keeping. But at every crucial point, we have found it missing. We have encountered much assertion, but no evidence. There is no longer a command to rest on Saturday, and there is none to indicate that the Sabbath was moved to Sunday. Sabbatarians cannot adequately counter the fact that the Mosaic code was abolished. They want to hold on to the stone tables that God took from them. Go back and read again about the failures of Sabbatarians to offer evidence.

Apart from Sabbath-keeping, how do the lives of those non-Sabbatarians who seek to faithfully observe all that Christ commanded (Matthew 28:20) differ spiritually from Sabbatarians? Are they inferior as a consequence of not keeping the Sabbath? Among some who hold to the day-change view, frequently there is narrowness, legalistic thought, and severe judging of others. Can that be the fruit of the Spirit? We are to be a people "zealous for fine deeds" (Titus 2:14), a people who love one another.

It's time to count up the evidence for Sabbath keeping. It is as follows:

1. Biblical evidence that the Sabbath is for Christians 0

2. Biblical evidence that the Sabbath was changed from Saturday to Sunday 0

3. Biblical evidence that the Sabbath was a creation ordinance 0

4. Biblical evidence that the Sabbath was kept prior to Sinai 0

5. Biblical evidence that the Sabbath was given to anyone other than the Jews 0

6. Biblical evidence that the Sabbath is required in the New Testament................................... 0

7. Biblical evidence that the Sabbath was broken by New Testament believers 0

8. Biblical evidence that the Sabbath day was set aside as a Christian holy day............................ 0

9. Biblical evidence that the Sabbath was kept by the apostles....................................... 0

Total biblical evidence for Sabbath keeping by Christians... 0

Whatever your present inclination with regard to the Jewish Sabbath may be, I trust that after having read this book, you will not disparage any of Christ's commandments but will, rather, do all that you can to understand, promote, and obey them – *as God intended* (the italics are important). Now, may God's Spirit work in your heart through His Word that you may find saving, sanctifying, and glorifying rest in the Lord Jesus Christ – both now and forever.